EVERY DAY

with

Jesus

DEVOTIONAL

God Loves and Cares for You

SHIRLEY A. HOWARD

Writers'
BRANDING

ISBN: 978-1-63945-272-9 (Paperback)

        978-1-63945-273-6 (Ebook)

The views expressed in this book are solely those of the author and do not necessarily reflect the views of the publisher, and the publisher hereby disclaims any responsibility for them.

Writers' Branding

1800-608-6550

www.writersbranding.com

orders@writersbranding.com

THIS JOURNAL BELONGS TO

_____

From

_____

Date

_____

INTRODUCTION

This journal was birthed out of a deep, heartfelt desire to encourage family members, friends, and readers who face daily challenges and extreme difficulties.

With this journal, I aim to help the reader develop an intimate relationship with God and to help those who already know Him to become much closer. And for me, it is a call to obey the Lord: "What I have invested in you, invest in others."

As an ordained minister, I strongly believe in the power of God, which works through faith and obedience to His Holy Word. And as we commune with the Lord in daily prayer, Bible study, and obedience, we develop a deeper relationship with Him that spiritually moves us to truly know that God loves and cares for us.

Over the years, I have preached the Word of God, taught numerous Bible classes, and conducted seminars on prayer and Christian living, both locally and in other states.

I am actively involved in local and district Christian education in Ohio. And for a number of years, I served as a teacher and also as the dean of Christian education for the Progressive Baptist Association in Cleveland, Ohio. I currently serve as an instructor.

I also teach a weekly Wednesday-evening Bible class at Mt. Zion Baptist Church in Lorain, Ohio. And I attend a Tuesday- and Thursday morning Bible class, where I teach twice each month.

I have a Master's of Education degree from Cleveland State University in Cleveland, Ohio. I hold a master's degree in Clinical Pastoral Counseling and a Doctor of Ministry degree from Ashland Theological Seminary in Ashland, Ohio.

I close by briefly sharing my personal experience as to why I chose the title *Every Day with Jesus* and the subtitle *God Loves You, and He Cares.*

For seven years, I went through a very emotional and stressful situation that forced me to rely on the Word of God and prayer in order to emotionally and spiritually survive. It was through this experience that I learned firsthand that *Every Day with Jesus* was the only way I would survive and thrive. The daily study of God's Word, prayer, and meditation sustained me emotionally, mentally, and spiritually. It was through this ordeal that I discovered that God really loves me and He cares deeply.

This journal may be used daily as a morning, midday, or evening pick-me-up to provide spiritual insight for your quiet time with the Lord. It can also be used in a group study setting for discussion and sharing, if you desire.

Ideally, if time allows, it is most beneficial to read, study, and meditate on the Word during the morning hours while your mind is clear and not cluttered by the challenges of the day.

As you read through these pages, it is my prayer that you will be drawn closer to the God that I love and to the One who loves us more than our finite minds can comprehend.

My desire and hope is that you will love Him more and intimately experience God's love and care as you commune every day with Jesus.

Respectfully and gratefully submitted,

Shirley A. Howard

In this journal, you will discover five nuggets for your day:

1. A title theme for each day

2. Words to grab your attention

3. A scripture to ground your thoughts

4. A brief explanation of scripture to guide your heart

5. A prayer of meditation to help you center and focus on God's provision

In addition, space is provided for daily thoughts and reflections, and each month you will find words of poetry and a scripture to further provide peace and calm for your spirit and soul.

Behold, I make all things new.
—Revelation 21:5 (NIV)

HAPPY NEW YEAR

It's a new day and a new year.
The outcome of it is not clear—
But I will not fear, because Christ
My Savior I revere!

A brand-new year and a new day!
I bow down on my knees to pray:
"Lord, thank You for another year
And another day!"

For down through the years, I've
Learned that Your grace and
Mercy are here to stay!

Happy New Year is what I say
With gratitude for each passing
Day!

Shirley A. Howard

JANUARY

Cast all your anxieties on him because he cares for you.
—1 Peter 5:7 (NIV)

GOD LOVES YOU, AND HE CARES

God loves you, and He cares,
And His grace and mercy He shares.
So wayward hearts He prepares!

God's love is amazing.
Curious eyes keep on gazing
As new trails, the Gospel message, continue
Blazing!

God loves you, and He cares
More than you will ever know,
For His desire for you is that you will grow.
So day by day, more love allow Him to bestow!

For the Lord cares, as He sits high and looks
Down low!
He traces each step as you go!

In all things, you must know that the Lord cares
And He loves you so!

Shirley A. Howard

JANUARY 1: GOD'S LOVE

There is nothing that God cannot do, nothing
that He cannot see you through!

Jeremiah 31:3 (NIV) says, "I have loved you with an everlasting love."

When you take God's hand by faith, He will begin to reveal His plan for your life. Learn to trust Him amid the fear, pain, and tears. You may never know why things happen as they do, but you must believe that Christ loves you more than you can think or imagine. Look to Calvary, and you will begin to see.

Prayer

Dear Lord, I thank You for the first day of this new year. I come with some doubts and fears in my heart. But I know that You are God and that all power and healing rest in Your hands. Lord, You know my sorrow and pain and the anguish within my heart. Help me to know and understand who You are. Show me Your healing power and the purpose in all that I experience. I ask this in Jesus's name. Amen.

_____
_____
_____
_____
_____
_____

JANUARY 2: ENDURE

> As you endure, I'll give you a heart that's pure
> As you trust Me, you'll discover that My love
> For you is sure!

John 1:1–2 (NIV) says, "In the beginning was the Word, and the Word was with God, and the Word was God. He was with God in the beginning."

A new beginning is marked by a new year. Just keep trusting in Jesus Christ as you allow His Word to resonate in your heart. The more you learn of Him, the more you will experience His love for you. You must believe that it is through Christ that each victory is won. He is the Living Word from beginning to end.

Prayer

Holy Father, I thank You for this day of a new year. Teach me to trust You more and more as the days go by; this I ask in Jesus's name. Amen.

JANUARY 3: ENDURANCE

Lord, when you help me to mature, You also teach me to endure
And through Your Holy Word and prayer, my faith is made
sure!

Isaiah 43:2–3 (NIV) says, "When you pass through the waters, I will be with you; and when you pass through the rivers they will not sweep over you. When you walk through the fire, you will not be burned; the flames will not set you ablaze. For I am the Lord, your God, the Holy One of Israel, your Savior."

God sees and cares for you even when it looks and feels as if He doesn't. He is right by your side, waiting to be your guide. In the rivers of difficulties and trials, the Lord is with you and won't allow you to drown. And the fire of oppression and pain will not consume you because the Lord is with you. He will never leave you alone.

Prayer

Dear Lord, I thank You for this day. It's not all I desire it to be, but because I know You are with me, I can make it through one day at a time. Thank You for keeping me. Continue to encourage my heart in Jesus's name. Amen.

JANUARY 4: SEE MORE CLEARLY

> A New Year to see God more clear—the reading
> of God's Word and prayer draws me near!
> The Lord empowers me to handle the doubt and
> fear! So, I trust Him to wipe away each tear, as He
> shows me—to His heart, I am held dear!

John 3:16 (NIV) says, "For God so loved the world that he gave his one and only Son, that whoever believes in him shall not perish, but have everlasting life."

The Holy Word gives comfort in knowing that God's love for humankind has no limits or bounds. Not only does God love us, but He proved it by sending His Son, Jesus Christ, to die for our sins and rise from death. You must personally believe that Christ died so that your sins would be forgiven. Within your heart, do you know that God loves you unconditionally? Stop and observe the evidence of God's love in your daily life.

Prayer

Lord, thank You for sending Jesus to die for me. I know that You love me and that You care about what I'm going through. Because I live in a fallen world, I know there will be pain and suffering, but by Your stripes, I am healed. I claim Your healing today in Jesus's name. Amen.

_____
_____
_____
_____
_____

JANUARY 5: I CAN SEE

Today I can see that through prayer and the Word of God I'm being set free! I trust You to make me what You desire of me!

Proverbs 3:5–6 (KJV) says, "Trust in the Lord with all thine heart; and lean not unto thine own understanding. In all thy ways acknowledge Him, and He shall direct thy paths."

So often it is difficult to trust anyone, even the Lord. Sometimes, we forget that the Lord knows what is best for us. The Lord desires for you to trust Him completely (nothing doubting) in every choice that you make. I challenge you to carefully think and pray and then trust the Lord to lead you where He desires for you to go.

Prayer

Lord, calm my fears and dry my tears. Remove the doubts that creep into my thoughts. I don't understand the reason for all that occurs in my life, but I trust You to see me through it. Show and give me Your heart. Allow me to see things as You see them. Amen.

JANUARY 6: REJOICE IN THE LORD

Lord, today I bless Your name from the center of my heart.
I am grateful that You are my one true God!

Psalm 118:24 (NIV) says, "This is the day that the Lord has made;
we will rejoice and be glad in it."

There are days when the last thing we want to do is rejoice,
when our mood is down and our situation is out of hand, filled
with sorrow, pain, or guilt. But like the psalmist, we can be honest
with God about how we feel. Take a moment, and quiet your spirit
as you meditate on His goodness. Allow your heart to be filled
with thankfulness and praise.

Prayer

O Lord, I will rejoice in Christ my Savior. Thank You for Your
goodness and love, which I experience each new day that You give.
Teach me to rejoice and be glad in Your presence every day. Today,
I choose to rejoice and be glad! Amen.

JANUARY 7: LIFT UP MY HEAD

On the days that are filled with sickness and dread,
Lord, come alongside and lift up my bowed-down head!
Hold me close so I won't be afraid!

Psalm 145:14 (NIV) says, "The Lord upholds all who fall, and raises up all those that are bowed."

Sometimes your burdens seem more than you can bear. You may begin to wonder whether you will make it through. Be assured, in your heart, that God is able to lift you up above your circumstances. He is a Burden-Bearer and a Heavy-Load Sharer. Allow Him to teach you how to trust Him. Expect the Lord to bring you out.

Prayer

Lord, I trust in You. I rely on You to lift up my bowed-down head. I wait patiently and expectantly for Your healing touch. I cast all my cares and concerns on You, Lord. Help me to be strong today and face what I must in order to be victorious in Jesus's name. Amen.

JANUARY 8: MY SHIELD

> You, O Lord, are my Shield, and by Your Word,
> the arm of God's might is revealed!
> It teaches me that You are the God who is real and are touched
> by the sickness that I feel, so, praise and worship to You, I give!

Psalm 3:3 (KJV) says, "But Thou, O Lord, art a shield for me; my glory, and the lifter up of mine head."

When we face trials and tribulations, we feel like giving up. But, by faith, we hang in there when we are seriously let down by life because we know that there is one hope—Jesus Christ. We know that His glory will be seen through the things He has promised. God promised to be shield and buckler.

Prayer

Lord, thank You for Your provisions. Teach me how to live one day at a time; teach me how to forgive. Protect me from the enemy's snare by guarding my heart and mind against wayward thoughts, words, or deeds. Lord, shield me from negative thoughts from the enemy. Show me Your will for my life. Amen.

_____
_____
_____
_____
_____
_____

JANUARY 9: GOD HEARS ME WHEN I PRAY

Lord, when I pray, I am confident that You hear.
It is Your holy and righteous name that I revere.
I invite Your Holy Spirit to draw near!

Psalm 4:1 (KJV) says, "Hear me when I call, O God of my righteousness: thou hast enlarged me when I was in distress; have mercy upon me, and hear my prayer."

The psalmist cried out to God to hear his prayer. We also plead with Him to give relief in the midst of our distress. He alone is able to fulfill our greatest need. It is our trust in the Lord that assures us of His mercy toward us.

Prayer

Lord, I am thankful that you hear my faintest cry. I am grateful that you are touched by my infirmity and weakness. Lift me up when I am weak and feel alone. Reassure me that I am Your own. Strengthen me on every leaning side. Touch my body and take away the pain as You minister Your healing touch. I pray in Jesus's name. Amen.

JANUARY 10: LORD, HELP

Your grace and mercy is from everlasting to everlasting,
And in Your holy presence I am continually basking!

Psalm 6:2 (NIV) says, "Have mercy upon me, O Lord; for I am weak: O Lord, heal me; for my bones are vexed."

The Lord knows what we are going through, and He is touched by our pain and afflictions. He knows our weaknesses and shortcomings. He loves and cares for His own, and He has promised to be with us in all that we go through. Do you trust in the Lord?

Prayer

Lord, I thank You for Your love and care. You know my weaknesses, and You will keep Your promise to never put more on me than I can bear. I trust You to be with me in my weakest hour and uphold me with Your mighty hand of power. Heal my body, and be my strong, high tower. Amen.

_____
_____
_____
_____
_____
_____

JANUARY 11: A REFUGE IN TIMES OF TROUBLE

Jesus is my Hiding Place! He is my Protector
and Provider—my Jehovah Jireh!
I come before Him and fall at His feet. His
peace and power are my holy retreat!

Psalm 9:9 (NIV) says, "The Lord also will be a refuge for the oppressed, a refuge in times of trouble."

In times of trouble, do you seek your own council, or do you seek the council of others? There are times when we do seek the council of others, but seeking guidance from God is best. He knows what you need and can provide the proper solution for your problems. He offers relief from oppression and depression.

Prayer

Lord, thank You for being my refuge in times of trouble. Thank You for coming alongside and uplifting the burdens that press so heavily upon me. I am grateful and confident that You are always near and You care. Amen.

JANUARY 12: THE POWER OF WORDS

Lord, guard my heart and mind; give me
the heart and mind of the Divine!

Proverbs 23:7a (NIV) says, "For as a man (or woman) thinks in his heart, so is he."

Be careful what you think about. Be mindful of what you allow to linger in your mind/heart. Your thought life will affect everything that you do. It is very important to guard your heart/mind. Your thoughts determine your actions, and your actions will guide your destiny.

Prayer

Lord God, I am so grateful that I belong to You. I thank You for constantly watching over me. Thank You for renewing my mind and giving me Your heart. Show me how to cast all my cares on you in times of trouble and disappointments and in confusion and misunderstandings. Amen.

JANUARY 13: LIVING IN THE SPIRIT

> Lord, I desire Your mind and Your heart, so
> that my life is aligned with Holy God!

In 1 Corinthians 2:16b (NIV), we read, "But we have the mind of Christ."

No one can fully understand God, but by His Spirit, believers have insight into some of God's plans, thoughts, and actions. We have God's Word to enlighten us and prayer to strengthen and sustain us. Through the work of the indwelling Holy Spirit, we can begin to know God's thoughts, discuss them with Him, and expect God to answer our prayers. Are you spending time with Him in prayer, so as to have His mind and heart?

Prayer

Lord, I desire to know You in Your fullness. I desire all of You and none of me. Increase my understanding so that I will discern the voice of Your Holy Spirit. Tune my ear to hear Your voice in my daily walk. Train my heart to know the dictates of Your heart that I may obey Your will and walk in Your way. Amen.

_____

_____

_____

_____

_____

_____

JANUARY 14: I BELIEVE IN THE SON

> In the Son, our salvation was won; He died and rose from
> the dead so that our redemption would be done!

John 3:36 (KJV) says, "He that believeth on the Son hath everlasting life: and he that believeth not the Son shall not see life, but the wrath of God abideth on Him."

In order to have eternal life, Jesus says that we must believe in Him and receive His plan of salvation. Salvation comes when we believe that Jesus Christ is the true Son of God and we invite Him into our heart. Scripture assures us that we are saved as we seek to love and obey His commands. When we choose to follow Christ, we choose eternal life and experience the benefits of His unconditional love.

Prayer

Holy Father, I thank You for Your Son, Jesus Christ, who died upon the cross for my sins. He was buried and rose again with all power in His hands. He now sits on the right-hand side of Your throne in heaven and pleads my case. I thank You that I am saved and have the indwelling Holy Spirit living within. And I have confidence to know that You hear my prayers and will answer them in Jesus's name. Amen.

JANUARY 15: FAITH PLEASES GOD

Faith pleases God! It is the key to understanding His heart!

Hebrews 11:6 (NIV) says, "But without faith it is impossible to please him; for he that comes to God must believe that he is, and that he is a rewarder of them that diligently seek him."

Faith believes what God has said about Himself in His Holy Word, the Bible. It also believes what the Holy Spirit reveals concerning God through prayer and meditation as we seek to obey Him. In other words, faith is believing and obeying what God says. Is your life pleasing to God?

Prayer

Heavenly Father, thank You for Your faithfulness to me. Thank You for revealing Yourself through Your Holy Word, prayer, and the indwelling Holy Spirit. Lord, help me to strengthen my faith and trust in You by doing what You say, especially during the times when I don't understand why things happen as they do. Amen.

_____
_____
_____
_____
_____
_____

JANUARY 16: LET FAITH MOVE YOU TO IT

When you let faith move you to it,
Watch God move you through it!
To believe, trust, and obey is the only way!

Matthew 9:29 (NIV) says, "Then touched He their eyes, saying, 'According to your faith be it unto you.'"

Jesus didn't respond right away to the blind men's request to be healed. He wanted to see if they had faith. Sometimes people say they want God's help but don't really believe that God can help them. Do you believe that God can help you?

Prayer

Dear Lord, I thank You for loving me. I have faith and trust in You. I believe that there are no limits to Your power and abilities. I believe that if I have the faith, You can do the impossible in my life. Lord let Your will be done in my life today. Amen.

JANUARY 17: FAITH IS CONFIDENT AND CERTAIN

I'm confident that God is God and the Bible reveals His heart!
I'm certain that God will do what He's said, being our Sacred
Head!

Hebrews 11:1 (NIV) says, "Now faith is the substance of things
hoped for, the evidence of things not seen."

Faith has two components that serve as bookends—confidence
and certainty. By faith, we believe (are confident) in God's
character—God is who He says. We also believe in (are certain
of) God's promises—He will do what He says. In summary, faith
"believes a thing before you see the thing." Do you really have
faith in God?

Prayer

Lord, I thank and praise You for who You are. And because of who
You are, I am assured and certain that You will do what You say
exceedingly, abundantly, above all that I could ask or think. Thank
You for being You (the One True God). Amen.

_____
_____
_____
_____
_____
_____

JANUARY 18: GREAT FAITH

Great faith holds a special place in God's grace! God
is able to handle any problem that you face!

Matthew 15:28 (KJV) says, "Then Jesus answered and said unto her, O woman, great is thy faith: be it unto thee even as thou wilt."

The Gentile woman pleaded with Jesus to heal her daughter. Therefore, in spite of the problems of not being a Jew, she trusted Jesus to respond to her faith. Because of her unwavering faith, Jesus granted her request. He will do the same for us today. God is no respecter of persons. He responds to our faith. Do you believe?

Prayer

Lord, I am grateful that You are touched by my faith and trust in You. You know my heart and my needs. Grant my humble request according to Your divine will. This I ask in Jesus's name. Amen.

JANUARY 19: PUT YOUR FAITH IN GOD

Have faith in God! Trust and believe, and
give Him totally your heart!

Mark 11:22 (NIV) says, "'Have faith in God,' Jesus answered."

God can do anything, but He cannot fail. God will answer our prayers but not as a result of our positive mental attitude. It is our faith and trust in Holy God that removes the mountains of despair and troubles that arise in our lives. Prayer is the key that unlocked the door, but it is faith that allows the door to be opened to receive from the Lord. Allow your faith and trust in the Lord to lead you to a desired end.

Prayer

Lord, I thank You for being You—the Maker and Creator of everything. I believe in You, and I trust You because You are my blessed hope. My faith is not in the object of my request; it is in You, O Lord. I totally trust in Your omnipotent power and unfailing goodness. Thank You for hearing my prayer; I trust that the answer is on the way. Amen.

JANUARY 20: THE REASON FOR YOUR HOPE

Lord, I believe in Jesus Christ! I trust totally in
Him, and I put all my hope in Him.

In 1 Peter 1:3 (NIV), we read, "Praise be to the God and Father
of our Lord Jesus Christ! In his great mercy, he has given us new
birth into a living hope through the resurrection of Jesus Christ
from the dead."

This verse offers encouragement, joy, and hope through the
work of Jesus Christ. The Holy Spirit brings believers into God's
family through the redemptive work of Christ on the cross and
His resurrection from the dead. No matter what situation we may
find ourselves in, Jesus Christ offers hope that can never die when
we surrender to His will.

Prayer

Lord, I thank You for Jesus Christ and the working of the Holy
Spirit through God's redemptive plan. You give courage and
strength to press on in hope. Father God, thank You for the work
of Your Son. Amen.

_____
_____
_____
_____
_____
_____

JANUARY 21: PEACE WITH GOD

Praise the Lord; I have peace with our God!
He saved me and gave me His loving heart!

Romans 5:1 (NIV) says, "Therefore, since we have been justified through faith, we have peace with God through our Lord Jesus Christ."

It is because of Jesus that we now have peace with God, even though we may not be in a peaceful and tranquil situation. We are reconciled to God through Jesus's work on the cross. Peace with God comes only because Jesus paid the sin debt with His own blood.

Prayer

Lord, I thank You that I am accepted through the blood of Jesus by faith. Every situation and circumstance is covered by Christ's blood that was shed on the cross. I surrender my whole being to You, so that I might have peace that defies human understanding. Amen.

_____
_____
_____
_____
_____
_____

JANUARY 22: PEACE OF GOD

When peace like a river floods over my soul, I say,
"Thank You Lord for taking control."

John 14:27 (NIV) says, "Peace I leave with you; my peace I give you. I do not give to you as the world gives. Do not let your hearts be troubled and do not be afraid."

The indwelling Holy Spirit works in our lives to develop a deep and lasting peace that this world cannot comprehend. This peace is not limited by circumstances or situations; it is a confident assurance that the Lord controls all things. Therefore, we have no need to fear the future. We are empowered to face it with joyful peace.

Prayer

Dear Lord, I thank You for Your peace, which calm my fears and dries my tears. Your peace strengthens my heart and gives me courage when I feel afraid. Thank You for the blessed assurance that You are always near.

JANUARY 23: PEACE OF MIND IN GOD

In Christ, peace of mind is mine.
It is a gift from Jesus Christ, my Savior Divine!

Isaiah 26:3 (NIV) says, "You will keep in perfect peace him whose mind is steadfast, because he trusts in You."

In this world, we will have strife around us, but in Christ, we can know perfect peace even in turmoil because we trust in the Lord. We devote our lives to serving and pleasing Him by believing His Word and communing with Him in prayer. When we are pressed on all sides, we can know God's peace, which sustains us through all the trials we face.

Prayer

Lord, thank You for loving me unconditionally, for keeping me even when I turn away from You. And as my loving Father, You draw me closer to You. You assure me that You will not forsake me. Lord, I trust in You, hope in You, and rest in You. Lord, thank You for not giving up on me or allowing me to give up on myself. Amen.

JANUARY 24: NO NEED TO WORRY

Don't worry; trust, for believing in God, wholeheartedly is a must!

Philippians 4:6–7 (NIV) reads, "Be anxious for nothing, but in everything by prayer and supplication, with thanksgiving, let your requests be made known to God, and the peace of God, which surpasses all understanding, will guard your hearts and minds through Christ Jesus."

We all worry about one thing or another. But Paul's advice is for us to turn our worries into prayers. When we pray more, we will worry less. When you start to worry, stop and pray. The peace of God is not in positive thinking, in the absence of conflict, or in good feelings. Real peace comes with the assurance that God is in control of all things. Allow Him to have full control of your life. Entrust your family and all concerns to His capable hands.

Prayer

Lord, I thank You that no matter what happens in this life, good, bad, or indifferent, You are in control. You are with me and my family and will never leave me alone. You will always be near to guide, protect, and encourage me. You give me a heart and mind that's stayed on You. Thank You for Your daily presence, provision, protection, and peace. Amen.

JANUARY 25: CALM IN THE STORM

Your mind's thoughts may be tossed and driven as the wind
on an angry sea, but there is hope for your despair, joy for your
sorrow, peace for your worries, and relief from your pain.
—Howard, 14, "Inspiration for Life's Journey"

Mark 4:39 (NIV) says, "He got up, rebuked the wind, and said to
the waves, 'Quiet! Be still!' Then the wind died down and it was
completely calm."

The disciples panicked when the storm threatened to destroy
them. But storms come in different forms. We face various stormy
situations in life that cause great anxiety. We have two ways to
respond—we can worry and assume that God doesn't care, or we
can resist fear and put our trust in the Lord.

Prayer

Lord, I am so grateful that You faithfully calm the storms in my
life when they arise. Thank You for teaching me how to respond to
unexpected trials that assaults. I trust You to meet all my needs and
calm the fears and doubts that daily challenge my peace. Amen.

_____

_____

_____

_____

_____

JANUARY 26: GOD'S WILL IS ABOVE ALL

Not my will, Lord, but Yours be done; this
is the secret to each victory won!
All things are possible when we believe, and
if they align with God's purpose,
We will receive!

Mark 11:24 (NIV) says, "Therefore, I tell You, whatever you ask for in prayer, believe that you have received it, and it will be yours."

Our prayers are often motivated by our own personal interests and desires. Jesus prayed with the Father's interest in mind (Mark 14:36). He knew His Father's will. Therefore, when we pray, we should pray within God's will and with the expectation that He will answer our requests. The Lord's will is above ours. We must believe and not doubt when we pray. Believing prayer taps into God's power to accomplish the humanly impossible (Mark 10:27).

Prayer

Lord, let my will and desires align with Yours; then my prayers will be answered. Please give me Your heart and mind. I believe what You say and that there is nothing impossible or too hard for You. I resolve to trust and obey in every way. Amen.

JANUARY 27: ATTITUDE FOR SERVING

In hope, serve with joy and gladness! By faith, don't allow
your circumstance to bring sadness! Trust in the Lord!

Romans 12:12 (NIV) says, "Be joyful in hope, patient in affliction,
faithful in prayer."

True believers are joyful of their hope in Christ because He is
the basis of their rejoicing. Believers are steadfast in their endurance,
and they continue to pray for wisdom, guidance, and strength.
As they serve, they rely on God to order the affairs of their lives
and their families.

Prayer

Lord, thank You for the joy in my heart in whatever state I'm in.
Teach me to patiently wait on you to deliver me and my family
from the traps of the enemy. Today I live in hope that whatever
life brings, I will be able to overcome. Dear Lord, I ask you to
keep my family in your loving arms, as I patiently wait on You to
deliver us according to Your timing. In the name of Jesus Christ,
I pray. Amen.

JANUARY 28: OUR SOURCE OF HOPE

Put your hope in Jesus Christ, He's the only One who could pay sin's price. He died and rose again to give eternal life!

Psalm 39:7 (NIV) says, "But now, Lord, what do I look for? My hope is in You."

People spend much of their lives acquiring material things for earthly living. They give little thought to eternal things. David recognized that his only hope is in the Lord. What do you desire? Where do you place your hope?

Prayer

Lord, my faith and hope is in Christ alone. Thank You for Your faithfulness by providing my basic needs and those of my family. I commit my whole life to You because I recognize that it is in You, dear Lord, that I live, move, and have my being. Thank You for being my blessed hope. Amen.

JANUARY 29: BE ON YOUR GUARD

Be on your guard, for your goal must be to develop a Christlike heart!

In 1 Corinthians 16:13 (NIV), we read, "Be on your guard (be diligent); stand firm in the faith; be men (women) of courage; be strong."

Paul concluded the chapter by urging believers to be diligent in carrying out the will of God. Don't waver in your faith. We are called to be mature in courage and strength, to walk by faith and not by sight. We are better able to stand in faith as we read and meditate on God's Word.

Prayer

Lord, teach and empower me to be strong and very courageous. Give me the strength to stand firm in times of trial and testing. Uphold me with the right hand of Your righteous power, and I will be able to stand firm. Amen.

_____
_____
_____
_____
_____

JANUARY 30: HEAR AND OBEY THE WORD

Hear the Word of God and pray, so faithful
to the will of God, you'll stay—
Practice this every day!

Romans 10:17 (NIV) says, "So then faith comes by hearing, and hearing by the Word of God."

The righteousness of Christ is credited to believers by faith. Hearing requires responding to the Word of God in a positive way by submitting to and obeying God. Hearing God extends beyond physical hearing. It is our understanding that allows us to believe with our heart what the Word of God says. It is God's truth that renews our thinking.

Prayer

Lord, give me a mind and heart to receive, study, and obey Your truth. Then give me a desire to share Your Holy Word with others. Teach me Your precepts and show me how to live a life that will bring You glory. Lord, I desire Your mind and heart. Amen.

JANUARY 31: FAITH GIVES ACCESS

By faith, you have access to God; trust and obey,
for He desires to give you a new heart!

Romans 5:2 (NIV) says, "By whom also we have access by faith
into this grace wherein we stand, and rejoice in hope of the glory
of God."

As a believer in Christ, you and I stand in a place of great
privilege (grace). Grace is God's unmerited favor extended to each
believer. As a believer, you are declared not guilty and are drawn
closer to Him. You are no longer an enemy of God; you are a friend
and child of God because of the ministry of Jesus Christ. As you
trust God and obey, faith opens the door to total access to God!

Prayer

Lord Jesus, I thank You for Your amazing grace and Your peace,
which surpasses all human understanding. I am grateful that Your
righteousness has been credited to me by faith. And it was the blood
of Jesus that took away my condemnation, so that I may stand in
Your holy presence. My faith and hope rests in Christ alone. I love
You, and I thank You. Amen.

FEBRUARY

Love the Lord your God with all your heart and with
all your soul and with all your strength and with all
your mind and love your neighbor as yourself.
—Luke 10:27 (NIV)

GOD LOVES

God's love never fails.
His grace and mercy will always prevail,
Even when trials and troubles sorely
Assail!

His Holy Word clearly tells—
Trust and obey, and be assured that
I'll keep you each and every day!

Read, study My Word, and continually
Pray, and you'll have what you say!
For by your side I will stay!

Trust Me, and don't doubt as you obey!
And My strength and power will fill your
Heart without delay!

Shirley A. Howard

FEBRUARY 1: PLEASING TO THE LORD

> In all that I do, Lord, I desire to please You
> So, train my heart and mind to glorify You!

Psalm 19:14 (NIV) says, "May the words of my mouth and the meditation of my heart be pleasing in Your sight, O Lord, my Rock and my Redeemer."

We all have secret faults that are not visible. David desired for the Lord to spiritually cleanse his thoughts, heart attitude, and actions. What comes forth out of the mouth is drawn from the wellsprings of the heart. Are your words and deeds pleasing to God?

Prayer

Lord, I thank You that Your grace covers all my sins. Forgive the wrong I do today and the things I should do but do not. Set a guard over my lips that I don't sin with my words, and let my actions glorify You. For only You know the true thoughts and intentions of my heart. Let all that I do and say be pleasing to You. Amen.

FEBRUARY 2: PRAY OFTEN

To command your day learn how to pray
So within the will of God, you'll stay!

Psalm 55:17 (NIV) says, "Evening and morning, and at noon, will I pray, and cry aloud: and He shall hear my voice."

Praying throughout the day is an excellent way to maintain the right priorities each day. Daniel prayed in this manner (Daniel 6:10), as did Peter (Acts 10:9–10). The prayers of the righteous are powerful. Prayer is an effective weapon against the overwhelming evil in the world. Never let a day go by that you do not talk to God about the concerns of your heart.

Prayer

Father, I thank You for the privilege of prayer and the blessed assurance to know that at any time, day or night, I have access to heaven's throne. I know that when I need You, You are just a prayer away. For when I call, You will hear and answer. Thank You for keeping me day by day. Amen.

_____
_____
_____
_____
_____
_____

FEBRUARY 3: PERSIST IN YOUR PRAYING

> There is nothing that prayer can't fix, but
> you must persist in your praying!

Luke 18:1 (NIV) says, "Then Jesus told His disciples a parable to show them that they should always pray and not give up."

When Jesus instructed His disciple to always pray, He did not mean endless repetition or long, thoughtless prayer sessions. Praying continually means to make prayer a vital part of your life and make your life a prayer while living in a world that needs a powerful influence. It is a deliberate, determined, and heartfelt request before God, always believing that He hears and will answer. As we persist in praying, we grow in character, faith, and hope.

Prayer

Lord, teach me how to pray effectively and with Holy Spirit power. Make me to know Your heart, will, and purpose for my life. Give me endurance power in prayer, so that I don't give up when the answer is delayed or not answered as I desired. Help me to recognize that You always have a good reason for all that You do. Thank You for Your faithfulness to me. Amen.

FEBRUARY 4: PRAY AND BE ALERT

God calls us to pray and be alert
So the tricks of the devil, we'll avert
And to the will and purpose of God, we'll convert!

Ephesians 6:18 (NIV) says, "And pray in the Spirit on all occasions with all kinds of prayers and requests. With this in mind, be alert and always keep on praying for all the saints."

The Holy Spirit trains the heart to pray continually and to be alert to changing situations in life. The Spirit provides various strategies for prayer. You can pray quick, brief prayers—make them a habitual response to every situation you encounter throughout the day. And you can pray more concentrated prayers for yourself, you family, and others as the need arises.

Prayer

Lord, give me wisdom and power to pray in the Spirit—out of a heart and soul that's indwelt, illuminated, and filled with Your Spirit. Give me the desire to be all You desire of me. Make me to hear Your voice and obey as I share my faith with others. Amen.

FEBRUARY 5: LEARNING TO PRAY

To learn how to effectively pray
You need to practice it every day;
Then you'll be empowered God's
Word to obey!

Luke 11:1 (NIV) says, "One day, Jesus was praying in a certain place. When He finished, one of His disciples said to Him, 'Lord, teach us to pray, just as John taught his disciples.'"

Jesus prayed on every major occasion in His life. He prayed at the time of His baptism and the choosing of His disciples (the Twelve). Jesus slipped away in prayer, and He prayed with others around Him. A disciple, impressed with Jesus's prayer life, asked Him to teach them to pray. Likewise, He will teach us to pray when we ask Him. Prayer is one of the most powerful tools that God has given the believer. Learn to apply it every day.

Prayer

Lord, thank You for the privilege of prayer. Help me to know and understand the power of prayer and its necessity for my life, family, and ministry. Let my life of prayer be an encouragement to others. Teach me how to pray, in Jesus's name. Amen

_____
_____
_____
_____
_____

FEBRUARY 6: FAITH AND PRAYER

Faith and prayer, what can compare?
Decide to forgive, so you'll faithfully live!

Mark 11:25 (NIV) says, "And when you stand praying, if you hold anything against anyone, forgive him, so that your Father in Heaven may forgive you of your sins."

A forgiving attitude, as well as faith in God, is essential for effective prayer. Standing in prayer was a common prayer posture during this time period. Prayer is a matter of the heart. The Lord knows what lies within us, and He helps us bring troublesome issues to the forefront. A Christian's obedience to forgive the offenses of others is directly related to God's forgiveness of his or her sins.

Prayer

Father, forgive me of all my sins and help me to forgive any grievances that I have against another person. Search my heart and make it pleasing to You; this I ask in Jesus's name. Amen.

_____
_____
_____
_____
_____
_____

FEBRUARY 7: LOVE FOR ENEMIES

> Love your enemies, and love your God,
> For it all equates to an obedient heart!

Matthew 5:44 (NIV) says, "But I tell you: love your enemies and pray for those who persecute you."

The Lord requires believers to demonstrate His love to their enemies. We are commanded to love them and pray for them because Christ loves them. A perfect demonstration of Christ's love for all people was on the cross when Jesus said, "Father, forgive them for they know not what they do." He requires us to develop His heart.

Prayer

Thank You, Lord, for being a God of love. Because of Jesus, I'm able to love those who mistreat me. Give me a heart of compassion and forgiveness, so that I will please You and bring honor to Your name. Amen.

FEBRUARY 8: PRAY WITHOUT RESENTMENT

Lift up holy hands because it's God's command;
Avoid anger and resentment in order to activate God's plan!

First Timothy 2:8 (NIV) reads, "I want men everywhere to lift up holy hands in prayer, without anger or disputing."

When there are discord and disputes among Christians, prayers are hindered. Our goal should be to have a right relationship with Christ. Holy hands signify an eternal cleansing on the part of worshipers. Broken relationships affect our ability to pray.

Prayer

Lord, train my heart to hear and seek Your will above all else, so that my prayers will be unhindered. Make my desires pleasing to You. Cleanse me so that I will seek to resolve anger and resentment against others. I ask these things in Jesus's name. Amen.

FEBRUARY 9: PRAY AND CONFESS SINS

> Confessing your sins is how community begins—
> With a change of heart from within!

James 5:16 (NIV) says, "Therefore, confess your sins to each other and pray for each other so that you may be healed. The prayer of a righteous man is powerful and effective."

A mutual concern for one another is a means to guard against discouragement and divisions. Personal confession and prayerful concern provide healing of the soul. Praying to God and confessing sins brings forgiveness from God and the development of more intimate relationships with others.

Prayer

Thank You for forgiving my sins. Teach me how to open my heart and extend love and compassion to others. Show me how to pray for the needs of other. And as I pray for their needs, may my own needs be met. Heal my body, soul, and spirit in Jesus's name. Amen.

_____
_____
_____
_____
_____
_____

FEBRUARY 10: HOLY SPIRIT, PRAY FOR ME AND WITH ME

Holy Spirit pray for me
Reveal the things I cannot see
As You mold me into what I ought to be!

Romans 8:26 (NIV) says, "In the same way, the Spirit helps us in our weakness. We do not know what we ought to pray for, but the Spirit Himself intercedes for us with groans that words cannot express."

We are not left alone in our suffering or conflict, the Holy Spirit helps us in our weakness (physical, emotional, and spiritual disabilities). When we don't know how to pray or what words to say, the Holy Spirit prays with us by interpreting our prayer requests to God in a language that our words cannot express.

Prayer

Thank You, Lord, for aiding me in my moments of suffering and confusion. I am grateful that I don't have to worry or be fearful of the future. Sweet Holy Spirit, plead my cause according to the will of God the Father. I trust that His perfect will is being accomplished in my life. In the name of Jesus, I pray. Amen.

_____
_____
_____
_____
_____
_____

FEBRUARY 11: GOD WORKS ALL THINGS FOR GOOD

With God, all things work together for good.
This concept is not readily understood,
But it is a reality for those who belong to the Hood!

Romans 8:28 (NIV) says, "And we know that in all things God works for the good of those who love Him, who have been called according to His purpose."

God works out all things for our good. This does not mean that all things that happen to us will feel good. Evil is present in this fallen world, yet God is able to turn things around for our long-term good. His primary goal is not to make us happy, but to nurture and grow us to become conduits of His love and grace to others. This is how we fulfill His purpose.

Prayer

Lord, thank You for the confidence that I have developed in You. I know that wherever life takes me, it will work out for good, even though it may not feel good to me. I trust You in all that I do. I cast all my cares on You. I thank You for the assurance of Your love. Amen

FEBRUARY 12: MORE THAN A CONQUEROR

Lord, I am more because You made me more.
Jesus Christ opened salvation's door.
Now peace and joy are what's in store!

Romans 8:37 (NIV) says, "No, in all these things we are more than a conqueror through Him who loved us."

In Christ, we are able to overcome all adversities. Nothing can separate us from God's love. Because Christ overcame all, we too are overcomers. We are not just a conqueror; we are more than a conqueror. This means that God's power continues to enable us to keep on being conquerors to a greater degree, so that we will continue winning glorious victories through Christ.

Prayer

Lord, I thank You that You made me more than a conqueror. Whatever the situation in life, You've given me the power to overcome it. The victory is in Jesus Christ. Amen.

FEBRUARY 13: WHEN YOU CALL, HE WILL ANSWER.

When you call, God will answer you.
Each trial, He will see you through.
And in times of trouble, He'll rescue!

Psalm 91:15 (NIV) says, "He will call upon me, and I will answer him; I will be with him in trouble, I will deliver him and honor him."

The Lord promised to be with us, to rescue us from danger; to protect us from harm, and to honor and satisfy us because we belong to Him. We have the privilege in prayer to call on the Lord and be assured that He will answer. It is also true that He may not answer in a way that we expect or want Him to. So, we learn to rest in the truth that God is sovereign, and He responds to our needs with gracious love.

Prayer

Lord, I thank You for the blessed assurance of knowing that when I pray, you hear me and you will answer. Thank You for the confidence in knowing that You are with me and will deliver me from my troubles. Amen.

FEBRUARY 14: BLESSED THROUGH TRUTH AND HOPE

You are blessed by your trust in God,
For He alone can fulfill your deepest desires
And bring hope to the heart!

Jeremiah 17:7 (NIV) says, "Blessed is the man that trusts in the Lord, and whose hope is in the Lord."

A righteous man or woman is blessed because his or her confidence (trust) is in God. He alone is able to fulfill heartfelt needs and hopes. When we trust the Lord, we place the outcome of life situations in His hands.

Prayer

In You, O Lord, I am blessed and highly favored. Thank You for Your faithfulness and Your kind care toward me and my family. In all things, I know You are there to direct my steps in Jesus's name. Amen!

FEBRUARY 15: SAVED BY HOPE

Saved by hope because the blood of Jesus is the antidote!

Romans 8:24 (NIV) tells us, "For in this hope we were saved. But hope that is seen is no hope at all. Who hopes for what he already has?"

Paul maintains that salvation is both present and future. At the very moment that we believe in Christ, we are saved. Those who respond by faith to God's promise have hope—a confident expectation of bodily redemption or resurrection. And in our daily life, we are able to maintain a steadfast hope that God's Word is true and reliable.

Prayer

Lord, I thank You for the confidence in knowing that what You have ordained in eternity past will surely become a present reality. For what You say will be accomplished in Jesus Christ my Blessed Hope. Amen

FEBRUARY 16: HOPEFUL PRAISE

> My hope is expressed in my praise! To God
> be the glory with both hands raised!

Psalm 71:14 (NIV) says, "But as for me, I will always have hope;
I will praise You more and more."

As time passes, we recognize that the Lord has been our
constant help in the past. We never despair because we know that
in all things, God will be there to sustain and keep us. Praise is a
weapon that allows us to remain hopeful in the midst of suffering
and hardship.

Prayer

Lord, I thank You for the hope that fills my heart right now. I will
praise You all my days; in Your goodness and righteousness, I stand
truly amazed. Amen.

FEBRUARY 17: PREPARE FOR HOLINESS

> Prepare your mind, heart, and will, so that the
> grace and hope of God can be revealed.

In 1 Peter 1:13 (NIV), we read, "Therefore, prepare your mind for action; be self-controlled; set your hope fully on the grace to be given you when Jesus Christ is revealed."

We must be prepared for action through obedience, which is a conscious act of the will. We strive to be self-controlled by being free from every form of mental and spiritual excess. Holy living demands being directed from within. When we allow the Holy Spirit to direct us, we become determined to live holy until Christ's return.

Prayer

Lord, prepare my heart to do Your will. Give me wisdom to know what steps to take. Grant me strength to persevere with a steadfast trust in Christ. I put my hope totally in You and rely on Your Spirit to orchestrate the affairs of my life. Thank You for Your grace, mercy, and love. Amen.

FEBRUARY 18: PEACE IN JESUS

Jesus is the Prince of Peace, our Blessed Hope
and the foundation of our belief!

John 16:33 (NIV) says, "I have told you these things, so that in me, you may have peace. In this world you will have trouble. But take heart! I have overcome the world."

Because of Christ's death, burial, and resurrection, we have peace through Him and victory over the things of this world. Because Jesus overcame the world, we too are overcomers and have power to live victoriously, in spite of the pitfalls of this world's system.

Prayer

Lord, thank You for the victory that I have in Jesus Christ. He is my peace that defies human wisdom. When trouble comes, I cast my cares on Him. He overcame the powers of this world, and has given me the power to overcome. I love you, Lord. Amen.

FEBRUARY 19: SUBMIT TO HIM

You are blessed to be a blessing. Submission is required for the testing!

Psalm 2:12 (NIV) says, "Blessed are all who take refuge in Him."

Submission to the Lord is the source of all blessing. Christ's rightful place is to be King of our hearts and lives. Give the Holy Spirit full control by allowing Him to sit on the throne of your heart.

Prayer

Lord, I surrender my all to You. I give You rightful access to my heart and grant You full control of my life. Teach me to do Your will. Amen.

FEBRUARY 20: FORGIVE AND TRUST

When you forgive, mercy will live! Trust in God is a must!

Matthew 5:7 (NIV) says, "Blessed are the merciful for they will be shown mercy."

The merciful person extends mercy to others, and in so doing, she demonstrates God's mercy, which has been extended to her. She learns to forgive unconditionally.

Prayer

Thank You, Lord, for Your loving kindness and compassion toward me. Help me to show love and kindness to others, especially to those who are unloving and unkind to me. Amen.

FEBRUARY 21: OPPORTUNITY

All you need, God has given! And by His
grace and mercy you must be driven!

Proverbs 3:26 (NIV) reminds us, "The Lord will be your confidence and will keep your foot from being caught."

Trust the Lord and develop the gifts that He has deposited within you. Walk in the path He has for you, and He will guide your steps. God has given us the Holy Word and the privilege of prayer to provide a sure footing.

Prayer

Lord, all that I am rests in You. You are the source of my confidence, and I trust You to order my steps in Your Word all the days of my life. Thank You for keeping me. Amen

FEBRUARY 22: HOP THROUGH IT

> Your faith will move you to it, but without
> works, you'll never hop through it!

Hebrews 10:35 (NIV) says, "Do not throw away your confidence; it will be richly rewarded."

Christ is our Confidant, and our confidence rests in Him; therefore, we dare not quit or give in. We must persevere in our pursuit to carry out the divine assignment if we want to receive the prize that's promised by God.

Prayer

In You, O Lord, I will persevere in order to achieve what you have assigned my hands to do. Thank You for the confidence in doing Your will, so that I may receive the eternal promise and bring glory to Your name. Amen

FEBRUARY 23: PRAISE THE LORD

God is my Fortress and my Rock! I will praise
and worship Him around the clock!

Psalm 144:1–2 (NIV) says, "Praise be to the Lord my Rock, who
trains my hands for war, my fingers for battle. He is my loving
God and my fortress, my stronghold and my deliverer, my shield,
in whom I take refuge, who subdues peoples under me."

David looked back over his life and began to praise God for
each victory won. As did David, the Lord teaches us how to fight,
and He is our rock of defense and fortress against the enemy. Like
David, we too can say that the Lord is our protection in times of
danger. Let praise become your weapon and strong defense.

Prayer

Lord, thank You for all Your benefits. In every situation and
circumstance, You provided my needs. Thank You for giving me
endurance power and strength to press on in the midst of opposition,
sickness, disappointments, and oppression. You are my true God
and my wonderful provider. I yield my life to You. Amen.

FEBRUARY 24: STAY WITH GOD'S PLAN

Know God's plan; hold tight to His hand
as you obey His commands!

Jeremiah 29:11 (NIV) says, "For I know the plans I have for you, declares the Lord, plans to prosper you and not to harm you, plans to give you hope and a future."

The Lord encourages us to hold fast to His plan. He is our leader, guide, and protector. He encourages us to do what is right. Because He provides for us, we are able to fulfill His mission on earth when we remain committed to His plan. He provides boundless hope. This does not mean we will not have pain, suffering, or hardship; rather, it will provide assurance that God will see us through to a glorious conclusion.

Prayer

Father, thank You for Your plans and provisions for my life. My will and desire is to glorify You. I surrender my life and all of me to You. Thank You for loving me so much. Amen.

_____
_____
_____
_____
_____

FEBRUARY 25: GOD IS GRACIOUS

God is with you on your right side and on your
left side; all you need He will provide!

Isaiah 30:21 (NIV) says, "Whether you turn to the right or to the left, your ears will hear a voice behind saying, 'This is the way; walk in it.'"

The Lord is gracious to His people. He cares and works through situations in life to encourage and draw us to Him so that we will be sensitive to His Word. Believe and have faith in Him. Tune your ears to hear the voice of God as he speaks to your heart.

Prayer

Lord, help me to become more sensitive to Your Word. Make me to know Your plan and purpose for my life, to hear Your Word and be conscious of Your leading and guiding at all times. Teach me to pray and obey. Amen.

FEBRUARY 26: WHAT KIND OF FRIEND ARE YOU?

A true friend will be there to the end,
And when trouble comes, will stand to defend!

Proverbs 17:17 (NIV) says, "A friend loves at all times, and a brother is born for adversity."

There is a difference between knowing someone well and being a real friend. Loyalty is the greatest test to friendship. A friend will stand by you and help in times of distress or personal struggles. Are you only a fair-weather friend—you stay around when it benefits you? Jesus is the best friend to have. He will hear you when you call and will be there to catch you before you fall.

Prayer

Lord, I thank You for being my true Friend. You know me better than anyone else. You will never abandon me or forsake me. Help me to be a friend to others as You are to me. Amen

FEBRUARY 27: GIVE WHAT YOU WANT TO RECEIVE

When you give good things that you desire to receive,
it indicates that, in God's principles, you believe!

Luke 6:38 (NIV) says, "Give, and it will be given to you. A good measure, pressed down, shaken together and running over, will be poured into your lap. For with the measure you use, it will be measured to you."

This verse teaches that we reap what we sow. The same measure by which we give to others is the same measure by which we will receive. Certain attitudes and actions often reflect back on the individual. Do you give away what you don't want, or do you give what is valuable to you? Love should be the motive for all we do.

Prayer

Lord, help me become more giving, forgiving, kind, and loving toward others and less judgmental. Allow me to develop Your character and acts of compassion toward others. Amen.

_____

_____

_____

_____

_____

_____

FEBRUARY 28: BE A BLESSING

Each trial becomes a test, and each one gives an opportunity to bless!

Genesis 12:2 (NIV) says, "I will make you into a great nation and I will bless you; I will make your name great, and you will be a blessing."

God made this promise to Abraham. But he had to obey God in order to receive the blessing. He had to move out of his comfort zone and go to a place where God would show him. Are you willing to move out of your comfort zone for the Lord? Perhaps God is leading you to a place of greater service and blessing to others. Don't let your present position cause you to miss God's plan for you. Trust the Lord and obey the leading of the Holy Spirit.

Prayer

Thank You, Lord, for blessing my life. Show me how I may be a blessing to others each day. Thank You for keeping me each hour of the day. You encourage and strengthen me in my weakest hour. I am so grateful for all that You do. Amen.

FEBRUARY 29: HOPE, JOY, AND PEACE

Through faith, hope, joy, and peace will
be your soul and spirit, release!

In Romans 15:13 (NIV), we read, "May the God of hope fill you with all joy and peace as you trust in Him, so that you may overflow with hope by the power of the Holy Spirit."

Our God is the God of hope. He fills us with all joy and peace. Joy relates to the delight of anticipation in seeing one's hopes fulfilled. Peace results from the assurance that God will fulfill those hopes. Therefore, we experience joy and peace as we put our trust in the Lord. Allow the Holy Spirit to fulfil His purpose in your life.

Prayer

Thank You for the peace and joy that You give and the overflowing hope through the power of the Holy Spirit. You empower me to live a life that is pleasing to you, even in times of great trials and testing. Amen.

_____
_____
_____
_____
_____
_____

MARCH

Be not afraid, only believe.
—Luke 5:36 (NIV)

YOU'VE GOT TO BELIEVE

You've got to believe so God's grace
And mercy you'll receive!

Dwell in a faith that moves mountains
Out of your way!

And in God's Word and a prayerful state
Learn to meditate each and every day!

A faith that rests in God is an unwavering
Trust!
And it's possible because the Holy
Spirit lives in us!

You've got to believe in order to uproot
Problems in your life!
Remember that Jesus paid the price!
He opened the door to paradise!

You've got to believe to receive eternal
Life, for abundant life is now!

Shirley A. Howard

MARCH 1: A SIMPLE PERSON VERSUS A WISE PERSON

By faith you must believe God
So the heart can conceive what is of God

Proverbs 14:15 NIV tells us, "A simple man believes anything, but a prudent man gives thought to his steps."

This proverb compares the foolish and the wise person. The foolish person is gullible and naïve and is easily influenced by the distractions around him or her. He or she often does not think before acting. The wise person, in contrast, thinks before she or he acts by considering the consequences of her or his actions. Faith in God will cause one to pray before making decisions or taking action, so as to discern God's guidance and direction in matters of daily life. Do you inquire of God before acting?

Prayer

Lord, teach me Your wisdom. Give me spiritual discernment to make wise and prudent choices that are pleasing to You. Train me to seek Your will and purpose for my life, so that my desires are in alignment with Yours. Amen.

_____
_____
_____
_____
_____
_____

MARCH 2: CHRIST IS OUR STRENGTH

Christ is our strength, and He forgives the sins of all who repent!

Second Corinthians 4:16 (NIV) says, "Therefore, we do not lose heart. Though outwardly we are wasting away, yet inwardly we are being renewed day by day."

It's easy to give up because of problems within ourselves, in our relationships, or at work. And over time, we may feel like walking away. But rather than giving up, Paul focused on experiencing the inner strength from the Holy Spirit (Ephesians 3:16). We must not allow fatigue, pain, or criticism to cause us to lose focus of purpose. In our weakness, we must allow the resurrection power of Christ within to strengthen us moment by moment. Trials teach us to rely on His strength rather than our own.

Prayer

Lord, I thank You that I am renewed day by day because of Jesus Christ and the Holy Spirit, who dwells within. Help me to respond to adversity in a way that will grow and strengthen my inner being. Amen.

MARCH 3: CHRIST IS ALL WE NEED

Humble yourself and let Christ lead, for Jesus is all that you need!

In 2 Peter 1:3 (NIV), we read, "His divine power has given us everything we need for life and godliness through our knowledge of Him who called us by His own glory and goodness."

Everything the believer needs, Christ has provided through His death and resurrection. When we are born again, God, by His Spirit, empowers us with His own moral goodness. Because we are developing His heart and mind-set, we are able to live in victory according to the knowledge He imparts in us.

Prayer

Thank You, Jesus, for giving me all that I need for life and godliness through faith and trust in You. Help me to show forth Your goodness and glory to others, so they too may be saved and become recipients of Your glorious power. Amen.

_____

_____

_____

_____

_____

_____

MARCH 4: GOD'S GRACE IS SUFFICIENT

God's grace is sufficient for me; Jesus, by
the Holy Spirit, has set me free!

Second Corinthians 12:10 (NIV) says, "Therefore, I take pleasure in infirmities, in reproaches, in necessities, in persecutions, in distresses for Christ's sake; for when I am weak, then am I strong."

When we are strong in our own abilities or resources, we are tempted to do things our own way, which leads to pride. When we are weak, allowing the Lord to fill us with His power, we become stronger than we ever could be on our own. Humility allows us to be weak in selfish pursuit but strong in the power of God, who works in and through us to do His good pleasure.

Prayer

I thank You, Lord, that in whatever state I'm in, I trust You to see me through it. In my weakest hour, I find strength in Your power that works in me through the Holy Spirit. I realize that my strength lies in You and not in my own understanding. I yield to Your will, O God. Amen.

_____
_____
_____
_____
_____

MARCH 5: I'M CRUCIFIED, YET I LIVE

I'm crucified or dead in Christ, yet I live
For, in Christ, all my sins, He chose to forgive!

Galatians 2:20 (KJV) says, "I am crucified with Christ; nevertheless I live; yet not I, but Christ liveth in me; and the life which I now live in the flesh I live by faith of the Son of God, who loved me and gave Himself for me."

Legally, because of Calvary, God sees us as if we had never sinned. Because our sins died with Jesus Christ, we are no longer condemned. Relationally, we have become one with Christ. Our Christian life began when, in unity with Him, we died to our old life. We must die daily to our old sinful desires that keep us from following Christ.

Prayer

I thank You, Lord, that I no longer live, because You live in and through me. My old self died when Your Spirit came alive within me. Thank You for saving my soul. Help me to let Christ be seen in me daily. Amen.

MARCH 6: HUMILITY PAYS

Humility pays as I resolve to serve the Lord all my days!

First Peter 5:6-7 (KJV) says, "Humble yourselves, therefore under the mighty hand of God, that He may exalt you in due time: Casting all your cares upon Him; for He careth for you."

Too often, we worry about our position and status, hoping that we get recognition. But we must remember God's recognition is more important than human praise. God will bless us according to His own timing. When we obey, we are assured that regardless of present circumstances, in His time, He will lift us up. However, we do not obey Him just to be promoted or blessed by Him. We obey Christ because of our love for Him.

Prayer

Lord, I humbly submit my life to You. Every care and concern, I lay at Your feet. All that I am or ever hope to be is because of You. I trust You and turn over the reins of my life into Your hands. Thank You for caring for me. Amen.

_____

_____

_____

_____

_____

_____

MARCH 7: BE BRAVE

Because Christ rose from the grave,
We have power to be brave!

Joshua 1:9 (NIV) says, "Have I not commanded you? Be strong and of good courage; do not be afraid, nor be dismayed, for the Lord your God is with you wherever you go."

We are commanded to be strong and to have courage in the things that we face or have to go through in life. We are able to stand because of the promise of God's presence with us and in us. We may face many challenges in this life, but we have the blessed assurance that His presence and power are always with us and in us.

Prayer

Lord, You are with me, and Your power rests within my heart through Your Holy Spirit. I have faithful confidence that You will provide all that I need. Thank You for Your faithfulness to me. Amen.

_____
_____
_____
_____
_____
_____

MARCH 8: NEVER FORSAKEN

> On the cross of Calvary our sins were taken,
> so that by God, we're never forsaken!

Matthew 27:46 (NIV) says, "About the ninth hour Jesus cried with a loud voice, saying: 'Eloi Eloi lama sabachthani?' Which means, 'My God, my God, why have you forsaken me?'"

Jesus quoted from Psalm 22, which was an expression of the deep anguish He felt when He took on the sins of the world. It caused Him to be separated from His Father. Jesus's physical agony was horrific but worst of all was the spiritual separation from His Father. Jesus was separated from His Father so that we would never have to experience eternal separation from God. Without Jesus, where would you be?

Prayer

Lord, thank You for Your Son, Jesus, who died and rose from the dead so that I would never experience separation from the Father. Because of Jesus, I'm eternally saved. Amen

MARCH 9: RULE FOR SUCCESS

The rule for success is the sure formula to
be blessed! Abundantly blessed!

Joshua 1:8 (NIV) says, "Do not let this Book of the Law depart
from your mouth; meditate on it day and night, so that you may be
careful to do everything written in it. Then you will be prosperous
and successful."

This scripture contains a formula or rule for success from God's
perspective. The world's view of success is vastly different from
God's. His view of success is based on His power through His Word.
Success from God's view, according to this verse, requires three
things: not letting the Law depart from your mouth, meditating
on it day and night, and doing all that is written in it. Today, we
must speak, meditate, and study the Word continually, so that we
will be able to apply it to daily living.

Prayer

Lord, thank You for Your faithfulness toward me. I meditate on
Your Word daily; it will forever be on my lips and in my heart to
obey. Give me the desire and the strength needed to succeed. Amen.

MARCH 10: LET HIM BE YOUR DELIGHT

> Let God be your delight; then trust and expect
> Him to give victory in every fight!

Psalm 37:4 (NIV) reads, "Delight yourself in the Lord and He will give you the desires of your heart."

When you seek God before all else, He will give you the desires of your heart, because He becomes your heart's desire. To delight in the Lord means to have righteous desires and to trust in Him above all else. Does the Lord hold first place in your heart?

Prayer

Lord, you are the center of my joy. I desire You more than the things of this world. With my whole heart, I seek after You daily. Amen

_____
_____
_____
_____
_____
_____

MARCH 11: I LOOK TO YOU, LORD

With all my heart, I look to You, My Savior and God!

Colossians 3:23 (NIV) advises, "Whatever you do, work at it with all your heart, as working for the Lord, not for men."

In all that we do, it should be from the heart. A sincere heart is motivated by our love for God and is revealed through obedience. And the things we do are done to please God rather than to impress others. What is your motivation for what you do?

Prayer

Lord, in everything that I do, help me to do it with my whole heart out of gratitude and love for You. I desire to please You in all things. Amen.

MARCH 12: HOLD NOTHING BACK

> Lord, in You, my Rock, I hold nothing
> back; for in You, there is no lack!

In 1 Corinthians 15:58 (NIV), we read, "Therefore, my dear brothers, stand firm. Let nothing move you. Always give yourselves fully to the work of the Lord, because you know that your labor in the Lord is not in vain."

We are encouraged to stand firm in our belief in the principles of God's Word. Such a stand will encourage us to be faithful in service to the Lord as we fulfill our divine purpose. God has promised to reward us in the work that we do to advance His kingdom on earth.

Prayer

Lord, uphold me in service to You. In all that I do, let me put You first because You are always faithful to me. Show me what I must do to advance Your kingdom here on earth. Then empower me to carry out your will. Amen.

_____

_____

_____

_____

_____

MARCH 13: STANDING STILL

I stand still in all I face; I know Your love is real, and so is Your grace!

Psalm 46:10 (NIV) says, "Be still, and know that I am God; I will be exalted among the nations; I will be exalted in the earth."

The Lord calls us to trust in Him and not worry. He brings His peace in our lives as we draw near to Him in obedience. Because He is awesome, we proclaim His goodness wherever we go; and reverently honor Him and His power and majesty by how we live.

Prayer

Thank You for Your peace, which calms the storms within me. Teach me to take time each day to be still before You and exalt Your name to bless myself and others. Amen.

_____
_____
_____
_____
_____
_____

MARCH 14: I TRUST IN YOU

> I trust in You, God, for success,
> For Your will and way are the best!
> I believe in You—Your Word is true!

Nehemiah 2:20 (NIV) says, "The God of Heaven will give us success."

When troubles arise and oppositions oppose, it is imperative to be assured that the Lord is with us and will give us success. Success is not based on our own abilities, human resources, or personal genius. Our hope is in the Lord. Do you really trust the Lord?

Prayer

Thank You, Lord, for being on my side. And whatever the opposition or problem, all things are in Your hands. My hope and trust is in You alone. Amen

_____
_____
_____
_____
_____
_____

MARCH 15: NOT SHAKEN

Lord, I will not be shaken; for in Christ, I'm never forsaken!

Psalm 16:8 (NIV) says, "I know the Lord is always with me. I will not be shaken, for He is right beside me."

When you truly trust in the Lord, you'll know that He is on your side as you seek to obey Him. David knew God, and He was confident that God would be there. And since God was with him, he had no need to be shaken. We, like David, have no reason to be shaken when we put our total trust in Him.

Prayer

Thank You for the assurance of knowing that You are always with me. I have no need to be afraid or stressed out. Lord, You are by my side at all times; therefore, I will not be shaken by the troubles around me. Amen

_____
_____
_____
_____
_____
_____

MARCH 16: I BELIEVE IN GOD, MY CONFIDENCE

I rejoice in God; I surrender to Him all my heart!

Psalm 71:5–8 (NIV) says, "You have been my hope, Sovereign Lord, my confidence since youth. I will ever praise You. You are my strong refuge. My mouth is filled with Your praise, declaring Your splendor all day long."

The psalmist reaffirms his confidence in the Lord regardless of his troubles. He remembered that God was his hope, the One in whom he trusted from his childhood up to the present. Though others may not understand him, he continued to trust in the Lord. In good times and bad, we too learn to praise the Lord day by day.

Prayer

Lord, You are my strong refuge in times of trouble. All my life, You have been with me and ordered my steps. Therefore, I open my mouth to give You praise, and I'll give You glory all my days. Amen.

MARCH 17: STAND IN CONFIDENCE

> In confidence, I stand with God's mercy and
> grace streaming down from His hand!

Hebrews 4:16 (NIV) says, "Let us then approach God's throne of grace with confidence, so that we may receive mercy and find grace."

Prayer is the means by which we approach God. We can come boldly to God's throne of grace with confidence that He will hear and answer our prayers. We can come boldly and humbly with reverence because He is our Lord, Counselor, and Friend. We remember how He was with us and delivered us when trouble was all around.

Prayer

Dear Lord, I am grateful for the privilege to approach You in prayer with confidence, knowing that You hear and You will answer. Thank You for Your grace and mercy every day. Amen.

———————————————————
———————————————————
———————————————————
———————————————————
———————————————————

MARCH 18: TOGETHER IN THE LORD

When believers join together by faith,
The Lord will take haste
By providing His power and grace!

Matthew 18:20 (NIV) says, "Where two or three are gathered together in my name, there am I with them."

Conflicts among believers can be resolved in a way that pleases God when two or three who are filled with the Holy Spirit are willing to work together for the good of both parties. The Holy Spirit will give guidance and wisdom.

Prayer

Lord, thank You for Your wisdom and guidance in my day-to-day activities. Continue to order my steps by Your Holy Spirit as you give me insight in relating to others. Amen.

MARCH 19: UNSTOPPABLE WITH HIM

We are unstoppable in Him;
Christ gives victories that no one can condemn!

Philippians 4:13 (NIV) says, "I can do all things through Christ, who strengthens me."

No matter what Paul went through—"having a little or a lot"—he trusted the Lord. So, no matter what we have or don't have, our confidence must be in God's ability, not our own. It is through God's strength working in us that we are able to do the things that God commands.

Prayer

Lord, thank You for Your faithfulness. My confidence is in You. You give me strength and courage to go through each day. Every need You have promised to provide. Amen.

_____
_____
_____
_____
_____
_____

MARCH 20: IN GOD'S STRENGTH

With God's strength, I cannot fail,
For His grace and mercy will prevail!
And the walls of division will fall!

Psalm 18:29 (NIV) says, "In Your strength I can crush an army; with my God I can scale any wall."

David was confident in his trust of the Lord. He recognized where his strength came from. Therefore, he was assured that he could handle any problem or obstacle in his way. We too must have this kind of assurance in the Lord.

Prayer

Lord, I recognize that You are my strength and, in You, I can face anything that comes into my life. You give me strength to excel in all that I do. Thank You for being my God and my Provider. Amen.

_____
_____
_____
_____
_____

MARCH 21: ARE YOU FAITHFUL?

Be faithful to the end;
Trust and believe that He's working within
And is making you over again and again!

Hebrews 3:14 (NIV) says, "If we are faithful to the end, trusting God just as firmly as when we first believed, we will share in all that belongs to Christ."

There is nothing that can separate us from God when our trust and hope rest in Him. Jesus is our very best friend. He encourages, strengthens, and heals us. Don't doubt; just believe and obey, and then all God has promised will be yours!

Prayer

Mighty God, Everlasting Father, there is nothing You cannot do. Allow my faith to move me to what you desire of me. Help me to trust in You more and more each day. Amen.

_____
_____
_____
_____
_____
_____

MARCH 22: I WILL PREVAIL

Against all odds, my God will not allow me to fall apart
But will uphold my confidence with high regard!

Psalm 27:3 (NIV) says, "Though an army besiege me, my heart will not fear; though war break out against me, even then I will be confident."

Confident trust in the Lord says, "Even though I see no way out with my physical eyes, I will trust in the Lord." Our confidence must rest in Jesus Christ and what He did at Calvary. Do you believe what God says, or do you panic over what you see?

Prayer

Dear Lord, words cannot express my gratitude for all you have done and continue to do. I am so in love with You and thank You too. I trust Your Word, more than the situation that I'm in. I rest in Your mighty power to save. Amen.

MARCH 23: ALREADY DONE

The work began in me, I count it done!
Because my faith and trust is in the
Great and Mighty One—Jesus Christ is
His name, and His victory, I claim!

Philippians 1:6 (NIV) says, "Being confident of this very thing, that He who has begun a good work in you will complete it until the day of Jesus Christ."

We are never alone, for Jesus promised that He will always be with us. The Holy Spirit lives within us to lead and guide. The work that God has assigned for us, He will work it out. When we are in Jesus Christ, we are never alone.

Prayer

Lord, I am so grateful for Your constant provision. Thank You for never giving up on me. Amen.

MARCH 24: I DO WHAT HE SAYS

Lord, my goal is to do what You say.
Each day, I humbly pray,
Expecting You to make a way!

First John 3:19, 22 (NIV) tells us, "Our actions will show that we belong to the truth, so we will be confident when we stand before God ... And we will receive from Him whatever we ask because we obey Him and do the things that please Him."

Our faith is revealed by what we say and do. It must be built on God's Holy Word, which is faithful and true. In all that come or go, we must look to the Lord to provide for our needs. When we obey, we begin to be assured that God will come to our aid. He answers the prayers of the righteous.

Prayer

Lord, thank You for the blessed assurance of knowing that when I pray, You hear and will answer in Your time and as You desire. Amen.

MARCH 25: THE FAITHFUL GUIDE

> Lord, You are my Faithful Guide.
> You help me deal with my selfish pride
> And promised to never leave my side!

Micah 2:13 (NIV) says, "The Lord Himself will guide you."

The Lord is our Faithful Guide, and there is nothing that can keep Him from walking by our side. Every need He promised to provide, but we must totally and faithfully rely upon Him. His grace and mercy cannot be denied! Do you walk by faith or by what you see?

Prayer

Thank You for Your faithfulness even when I'm not faithful to You. Lord, I depend on You for each choice that I make and for each step that I take. Amen.

MARCH 26: THE WAY

You are the path I take, the truth I seek, and the life I make;
You keep me humble and meek!

John 14:6 (NIV) says, "I am the way and the truth and the life."

Jesus has covered every base in your life with Himself. He points the way that you must go. He is the truth that you seek and the life that you live. Trust and obey and do not doubt His power to heal. Because Christ is the way, we follow Him. He is the absolute truth, and from His life, we receive eternal life.

Prayer

Lord Jesus, You are everything to me. You are in my every thought; my dreams and hopes are in You. I trust in You and will forever cling to You. Amen.

MARCH 27: SHOW ME

Your Word shows me how to live;
It guides me in the life that I must give
And teaches me that I must love and forgive!

Psalm 25:4–5 (NIV) says, "Show me Your ways, O Lord, teach Your paths; guide me in Your truth and teach me, for You are God my Savior, and my hope is in You all day long."

The Lord is the revealer of knowledge and truth. He delights in revealing his nature and character to us. His goodness overwhelms us as He guides us day by day. He is our Savior, Wonderful Provider, Blessed Hope, and Healer of all our diseases.

Prayer

Lord, with my whole heart, I daily seek You. Let me never stray from Your truth. Thank You for Your goodness toward me. Show me how I may impart your ways in the lives of others. Amen.

MARCH 28: I WON'T STUMBLE

Your Word is my light, so I won't stumble,
And it is a guide to keep me humble!

Psalm 119:105 (NIV) reads, "Your Word is a lamp to my feet and a light for my path."

If we lose our way through the valley of discouragement, doubt, or self-pity, God's Holy Word is there to enlighten the path of our minds and hearts to lead us back to the path of obedient faith and trust in Him.

Prayer

Thank You, Lord, for being my light when my way grows dark. You walk with me, and sometimes You carry me. I praise You for who You are! Continue to be the Guiding Light in my life and in the life of my family. Amen.

MARCH 29: GUIDED BY HIM

Lord, my steps are guided by You! I put all
trust in You—the Faithful and True!

Psalm 119:133 (NIV) says, "Direct my footsteps according to your
Word; let no sin rule over me."

When we stand at a crossroad in life, we stop, pray, and seek
guidance from the Lord. When we trust in the Lord, He will
guide the path we take. Allow God's Word to order each footstep
on life's journey.

Prayer

Lord, You control the way I go. I surrender my all to You. I choose
to trace Your steps with my own as I follow Your lead. Thank You,
Jesus, that You supply all I need. Amen.

MARCH 30: CHILD OF GOD

The Holy Spirit is my Guide, and because I am His—
God provides and He walks by my side!

Romans 8:14 (NIV) says, "All who are led by the Spirit of God are children of God."

Children of God have no reason to worry or fret because the Father knows their needs, and He faithfully provides. Therefore, we learn to patiently wait and walk where He guides. Do you worry, or do you trust in the Lord?

Prayer

Lord, thank You for leading and guiding me by Your Holy Spirit. Give me attentive ears to hear and a faithful heart and steadfast mind to obey. Amen.

MARCH 31: BLESSED TO KEEP YOUR LAW

Lord, I'm blessed to keep Your commands and law
And with Your loving kindness You continually draw!

Psalm 119:2 (NIV) says, "Blessed are they who keep His statutes and seek Him with all their heart."

As believers, we always have a reason to love and praise God. We are a blessed people because we have faith in Jesus Christ. We trust in Him and obey His Word, realizing that without Him life ceases to exist.

Prayer

Father, thank You for caring for me. I delight in Your Word, and I trust You to guide my steps each day. And as long as there is breath in my body, I'll praise Your holy name with my whole heart. Amen.

APRIL

Peace I leave with you, my peace I give
unto you; not as the world gives.
—John 14:27 (NIV)

PEACE AND LOVE

Your peace and love came down
From above!

He was high, but He came low
So eternal life to all He would
Bestow!

Put your faith and trust in Jesus,
And He will help you spiritually
Grow!

Peace and love is what He gives.
It's available to all who will accept
His invitation to eternally live!

Peace and love is available to all!
Who will accept salvation's call?

Come to Jesus and be saved, for
By the shedding of His blood the
Road to eternal life was paved!

Shirley A. Howard

APRIL 1: TRANSFORM YOUR MIND

> To this world, I won't conform; I yield to Your
> Spirit to transform my mind to do Your will!

Romans 12:2 (NIV) says, "Do not conform any longer to the pattern of this world, but be transformed by the renewing of your mind. Then you will be able to test and approve what God's will is—His good, pleasing and perfect will."

As believers, we are called to resist the behavior patterns and customs of this world, which are often selfish and corrupting. Our refusal to conform to the world's values must go even deeper than our behavior and customs. It must be rooted in our mind and heart—"by the renewing of the mind." Only by surrendering to the Holy Spirit can we be transformed. The Spirit will teach us the will of God as we surrender to Him. We are called to transform the world with the truth of the gospel, not to conform to the world's philosophy.

Prayer

Lord, thank You for the work of the Holy Spirit in my life. I surrender my all to You. I give You permission to renew my mind so that I will know Your will for my life and obey it. And I will no longer conform to the world but will be empowered to transform it. Amen.

APRIL 2: BE WISE

> The man or woman who is wise trusts and
> relies on Holy God to advise!

James 1:5–7 (NIV) says, "If any of you lacks wisdom, he should ask God, who gives generously to all without finding fault, and it will be given to him. But when he asks, he must believe and not doubt, because he who doubts is like a wave of the sea, blown and tossed by the wind. That man should not think he will receive anything from the Lord."

Wisdom begins with respect and reverence for God, which leads to right living and discernment between right and wrong. A wavering mind is one that's not completely convinced that God's way is the best. If your faith is new, weak, or struggling, make up your mind to know that God is trustworthy. Doubt is like the wind, it will toss your mind and thinking to and fro. But you must let go and let God control your life.

Prayer

Lord, give me wisdom to know that there is nothing You cannot do. And if I put my trust in You and do not doubt, the seemingly impossible will be done in my life. Amen.

_____
_____
_____
_____
_____
_____

APRIL 3: BLESS THE LORD

I will bless the Lord, and in Him, I will rejoice!

Psalm 34:1–2 (NIV) says, "I will extol the Lord at all times; his praise will always be on my lips. My soul will boast in the Lord; let the afflicted hear and rejoice."

God has promised in His Word to bless His children. But many of these promises require our participation. He promised to calm our fears, dry our tears, deliver us from trouble, listen to our problems, supply our needs, and redeem our souls, but we must do our part by seeking and obeying Him.

Prayer

Thank You, Lord, for Your faithful provision and kind care. I will forever give You praise and thanksgiving, the fruit of my lips. Amen.

APRIL 4: WE MAY FAIL

We may fail, but God will prevail; the Gospel story, we must tell!

Luke 22:31–32 (NIV) says, "Simon, Simon, Satan has asked to sift you as wheat. But I have prayed for you, Simon, that your faith may not fail. And when you have turned back, strengthen your brothers."

Like Peter, we may fail because we miscalculate our own ability instead of trusting in the Lord. But Jesus assured Peter that his faith, although it would falter, would not be destroyed. His faith would be renewed, and he would be a powerful leader. The devil wanted to destroy Peter. Satan's desires have not changed, for he desires to destroy us also. Jesus has prayed for us too, and if we have faith, we too will be able to stand and strengthen others.

Prayer

Lord, thank You that even when I fail, You don't abandon me, but You strengthen and encourage me with Your Holy Word and the Holy Spirit with encouragement to press on by faith. Bless me with faith and courage so that I will be a channel of blessing for others. Amen.

_____
_____
_____
_____
_____
_____

APRIL 5: ASK IN HIS WILL

Whatever you ask in God's will, the Holy Spirit will fulfill!

John 15:7 (NIV) says, "If you remain in me and my words remain in you, ask whatever you wish, and it will be given to you."

When we remain in Christ, we bear much fruit. Effective prayer is based on faith in Jesus Christ and on His words remaining in us. His words must control our mind and heart so that our prayers conform to the will of God. When this occurs, we are sure that our prayers will be fulfilled. The key to answered prayer is that it must be within the will and purpose of Holy God.

Prayer

Let my mind and thoughts conform to Your will and way, so that whatever I ask for or do, will be pleasing to You. Amen.

_____
_____
_____
_____
_____
_____

APRIL 6: WHEN TWO AGREE

When two agree, whatever you ask for shall be!

Matthew 18:19 (NIV) says, "Again, I tell you that if two of you on earth agree about anything you ask for, it will be done for you by my Father in heaven."

Because the Holy Spirit resides in believers, the sincere agreement between two people in prayer is more powerful than the superficial agreement of thousands of people. Two or more believers who are filled with the Holy Spirit will pray according to God's will rather than their own. God will grant their request.

Prayer

Father, I ask You to increase my faith and trust in You. Teach me to know Your will and purpose as I pray and intercede for and with others. Let Your will be done in Jesus's name. Amen.

_____
_____
_____
_____
_____

APRIL 7: GOD, OUR ROCK

The Lord is our Rock and Protector, and our Provider and
Guide.
He's always near those who obey, and He is on their side!

Deuteronomy 32:30 (NIV) says, "How could one man chase a
thousand, or two put ten thousand to flight, unless their Rock had
sold them, unless the Lord had given them up?"

God wanted Israel to know that there is nothing impossible for
Him. He is able to do things that the human mind says is impossible.
And He can do such things in ways that we cannot comprehend.
The odds are always in God's favor. Faith and obedience are the
things that move the hand of God. Great is God's faithfulness to us.

Prayer

Lord, thank You for Your love and provision. You are able to do
things that we deem impossible. You are a miracle-working God.
I need a miracle right now. In Jesus's name, I pray. Amen.

_____
_____
_____
_____
_____
_____

APRIL 8: GOD'S MIGHTY WEAPONS

God's mighty weapons pull down strongholds, and
He provides nourishment for our souls!

Second Corinthians 10:4–5 (NLT) reads, "We use God's mighty weapons, not worldly weapons, to knock down the strongholds of human reasoning and to destroy arguments. We destroy every proud obstacle that keeps people from knowing God. We capture their rebellious thoughts and teach them to obey Christ."

Our God has given us weapons to use for the battle we must fight against the forces of Satan and evil. But we choose which methods to use, whether the ones God has given us or the ones man-made. God's mighty weapons are available to us in the form of—prayer, faith, hope, life, God's Word, and the Holy Spirit (Ephesians 6:13–18). These weapons break down the strongholds (proud human arguments) of the devil and tear down walls that keep us from trusting in God. The real battle is a spiritual one.

Prayer

Lord, thank You for Your provisions and the weapons to do battle with the enemy of my soul. All I need you have already provided. Teach me to use what you have given so that I will effectively serve others and bring glory to your name. Amen.

APRIL 9: I DON'T GIVE UP

I'll never give up, for in the presence of God, I sup!

Philippians 3:13–14 (NIV) says, "Brothers, I do not consider myself yet to have taken hold of it. But one thing I do: Forgetting what is behind and straining forward to what is ahead, I press on toward the goal to win the prize for which God has called me heavenward in Christ Jesus."

We all have made mistakes in the past. But we must not allow the past to control our present and future. We take with us the things of the past that will enhance our present and future. We look ahead and press to the goal so we can win the prize. Jesus Christ is the prize. Our trust, hopes, and dreams find fulfillment in our relationship with Him.

Prayer

Jesus, You are the prize that I seek. I will let nothing take my eyes off the prize. I seek Your plan and purpose for my life. Sweet Jesus, You are my life, my all in all. For only in You do I have everlasting life. Amen.

_____
_____
_____
_____
_____

APRIL 10: GOD'S INSEPARABLE LOVE

God's love has no limits or bounds! In my
ear, His melody of love resounds!

Romans 8:38–39 (NIV) says, "For I am convinced that neither
death nor life, neither angels nor demons, neither the present nor
the future, nor any power, neither height nor depth, nor anything
else in all creation, will be able to separate us from the love of God
that is in Christ Jesus our Lord."

In these verses, we have the blessed assurance from the Lord
that no matter how things look or what we feel, God is with us at
all times. And there is nothing that can separate us from His love
for us. In Christ, we are super conquerors (verse 37). His death on
the cross proved His love for us. As we believe these overwhelming
assurances, we will not doubt or be afraid to trust the Lord.

Prayer

Lord Jesus, I trust in You, and I hope in You. Each day, teach me
more and more to rest in knowing that you are near, for You live
in my heart. Amen.

APRIL 11: LOVE IS THE BOTTOM LINE

Loving God is the key, and His goal is for all to be free!

Second Peter 1:5–7 (NIV) says, "For this very reason, make every effort to add to your faith, goodness; and to goodness, knowledge; and to knowledge, self-control; and to self-control, perseverance; and to perseverance, godliness; and to godliness, brotherly kindness; and to brotherly kindness, love."

Faith is so much more than believing in certain facts. Faith means action. Growth in Christian character is a necessity for moral discipline and a truly transformed life. Faith allows us to know God better as we study the Word and pray and then apply what we learn about God. These disciplines are not options, and they require work and endurance on our part. The Lord empowers us, but we have the responsibility to learn and grow. Love, provides the fertile ground for productive growth.

Prayer

Lord, teach me the disciplines of taking time to grow my faith through the knowledge of Your Word and prayer. Help me put into practice each day all that I learn about Your goodness and unconditional love. Amen.

APRIL 12: GOD'S QUICK AND POWERFUL WORD

God's quick and powerful Word is to be heeded when heard!

Hebrews 4:12 (NIV) says, "For the Word of God is living and active. Sharper than any double-edged sword, it penetrates even to dividing soul and spirit, joint and marrow; it judges the thoughts and attitudes of the heart."

God's Word is more than a collection of words compiled in a book that we call the Bible. God's Word is living—having power to change lives by penetrating the thoughts and intents of the heart. It reveals truth—what we are and what we are not. It exposes lies and pretenses and gets to the core of our moral and spiritual life. God's Word reveals the good, bad, and ugly within us. Therefore, the Word requires that we change. We listen to God's Word and allow it to shape and mold our lives.

Prayer

Lord, Your Word is alive and powerful. It gives me strength to live and the power to face life challenges each day. Thank You for keeping me, for renewing my thoughts and infusing my heart with Your truth and love so I may help others. Amen.

APRIL 13: GLORIFY THE LORD

When you glorify God, you must do it with your whole heart!

Psalm 34:3 (NIV) says, "Glorify the Lord with me; let us exalt His name together."

This Psalm (song) of praise was written by David. He invites all believers to glorify the Lord with him. We are able to do it because, like David, we know the Lord is good to us. And when believers come together in corporate worship, of one accord, prayers are answered and miracles happen. Corporate praise sets the atmosphere for miracles to occur.

Prayer

Lord, I give You the glory and honor that's due Your name. You alone are worthy of all praise. Thank You for Your faithfulness and lovingkindness toward me and others. Amen.

APRIL 14: LOVE AND FAITHFULNESS

Love and faithfulness are expressed from a
heart filled with thanks and gratitude!

Proverbs 3:3 (NIV) says, "Let love and faithfulness never leave you; bind them around your neck, write them on the tablet of your heart."

God's love and faithfulness are expressed through His mercy and truth. He desires to see these character traits in us so that the world will get a glimpse of who He is. A faithful person believes God's truth and works to bring justice for others. The lives we live reveal who we are. God desires us to be loving, merciful, faithful, and truthful.

Prayer

Lord, You are loving, merciful, faithful, and true. Help me to be like You, so that I'll have Your mind, heart, and compassion to live each day in victory. Amen.

APRIL 15: PLAN WISELY

When you apply your hands, make sure
you're walking in God's plans!

Proverbs 16:1 (NLT) says, "We can make our own plans, but the Lord gives the right answer."

The final outcome of the plans we make is in God's hands. When doing God's will, there must be a partnership between our efforts and God's control. We can us our minds to seek the advice of others and to plan, but as we plan, we must seek God's guidance. God has ultimate control over all things.

Prayer

Lord, give me wisdom to make the choices that are pleasing to You. Amen.

_____
_____
_____
_____
_____
_____

APRIL 16: WHY DO IT?

Why do you do it?
Is it purely selfish, or does the Lord move you to it?

Proverbs 16:2 (NLT) says, "People may be pure in their own eyes, but the Lord examines their motives."

Individuals can rationalize anything if they have no standard for judging right and wrong. God's Word is the standard to use. Ask yourself three questions: Is this plan in harmony with God's truth? Will it work in real-life conditions? And is my attitude pleasing to God?

Prayer

Help me make decisions and choices that are in harmony with Your Word. Amen.

APRIL 17: DO IT FOR HIM

Do it for Him and not for yourself or them,
so that your heart won't condemn!

Proverbs 16:3 (NLT) says, "Commit your actions to the Lord, and your plans will succeed."

In all you do, put the Lord first. We must maintain a delicate balance of trusting the Lord as if everything depends on Him and at the same time, working as if everything depended on us. Give yourself wholeheartedly to God and His work.

Prayer

Lord, I give myself totally and completely to You. I hold nothing back. I seek to please You alone. Amen.

APRIL 18: WISDOM AND UNDERSTANDING

Wisdom is what we seek and understanding is
revealed by how we live and speak!

Proverbs 4:7 (NLT) says, "Getting wisdom is the wisest thing you
can do! And whatever else you do, develop good judgment."

Seeking God's wisdom is the most important choice we can
make. We can receive it as we seek to obey Him and by boldly
asking Him for it. God's Word is the wisdom we should seek first.

Prayer

Lord, give me wisdom to discern the truths in Your Word. Then
give me understanding to correctly apply them in my daily living.
Amen.

APRIL 19: GOD SEES ALL

> God sees all and is there to catch us when we
> fall; then He strengthens us to stand tall.

Proverbs 15:3 (NIV) says, "The Lord is watching everywhere, keeping His eyes on both the evil and the good."

At times, it seems as if God has let evil run rampant in the world. But God sees everything clearly—both the evil actions and the evil intentions lying behind them. He also sees the good. God cares, and He is actively involved in our world. We may not always see or feel His work, but by faith, we know He is working for our good. One day, the Lord will wipe out evil completely. What are you doing to help God in His work of righteousness?

Prayer

Thank You, Lord, for watching over my life. Nothing is hidden from You. You know the thoughts and motives of my heart. Let them be pleasing in Your sight as you teach me to live right. Amen.

APRIL 20: SEEK KNOWLEDGE

> Seek to know God; seek to understand His
> heart; then we won't soon fall apart!

Proverbs 15:14 (NIV) says, "The discerning heart seeks knowledge, but the mouth of a fool feeds on folly."

What we feed our minds is just as important as what we feed our bodies. The kinds of books we read, the people we talk with, the music we listen to, and the movies we watch are all part of our mental diet. We must be discerning because what we feed the mind influences our total health and well-being. Therefore, a strong desire to discover knowledge (God's) is a mark of wisdom. Feast on God's Word; apply it to your life daily.

Prayer

Give me a heart that seeks to know you better. Draw me closer to You, and enlighten my understanding of who You are. Thank You for the Word, which nourishes my soul and spirit. Amen.

APRIL 21: LIVE TO PLEASE

> When you live to please, the Holy Spirit will
> comfort you, and your troubles will ease!

Proverbs 16:7 (NIV) says, "When a man's ways are pleasing to the Lord, He makes even his enemies live at peace with him."

Sometimes, we put more effort into pleasing others than we do into pleasing God. We should put more energy into pleasing God, first and foremost. Seeking to be a peacemaker pleases God, and it will be beneficial for those around us. If it doesn't work, we lose nothing, yet we're still pleasing to the Lord—the only one who truly matters.

Prayer

Lord, teach me to seek You first in all that I do. Let my allegiance and devotion be to You first, above all others. Show me how to find balance in achieving this goal. Amen.

APRIL 22: THE LORD, YOUR TOWER

The Lord is the strong, high tower who gives power
to the faithful in their weakest hour!

Proverbs 18:10 (NIV) says, "The name of the Lord is a strong tower, the righteous run to it and are safe."

The righteous turn to the Lord based on who He is. There is none greater than He. They put their trust in the Lord, and in Him, they find safety. As our high tower, He keeps us from disaster.

Prayer

Thank You, Lord, for being my mighty high tower in the time of trouble. I completely trust in Your ability to save me. Amen.

APRIL 23: EXAMINE YOUR WAYS

Allow the Lord to guide your way!
Trust and obey Him day by day,
As You read and study His Word and daily pray!

Proverbs 21:2 (NIV) says, "All a man's ways seem right to him, but the Lord weighs the heart."

We may think that nothing is wrong with our ways of doing things, but the Lord knows our heart (innermost secrets). We see and judge things based on outward appearances, but the Lord sees the heart. He observes the true motives of the heart and judges them accurately. He sees all and knows all.

Prayer

Lord, teach me Your ways. Give me a desire to know You better and daily walk in Your truth. My desire is to please You. Amen.

_____
_____
_____
_____
_____
_____

APRIL 24: OBEY THE LORD

Live right, talk right, and trust the Lord, so each battle, He'll fight!

Proverbs 21:3 (NIV) says, "To do what is right and just is more acceptable to the Lord than sacrifice."

The Lord desires our obedience (doing what is right) more than our sacrifice. He does not approve of hypocrisy (say one thing and do another).

Prayer

Lord, help me talk right and live right. Because of Jesus, my worship and praise are genuine and from my heart. Please hear and answer my prayers. Amen.

APRIL 25: DAILY REJOICE

Each day you live provides an opportunity to make the right
choice—
Walk in faith, and obey God's voice!

Ecclesiastes 11:7–8 (NLT) says, "Light is sweet; how pleasant to
see a new day dawning. When people live to be very old, let them
rejoice in everyday of life. But let them also remember there will
be many dark days. Everything still to come is meaningless."

Solomon speaks metaphorically of light and darkness as figures
of life and death. He encourages us to enjoy life. We do this when
we seek to live each day at a time—live in the present. As we grow
old, it moves us closer to darkness. Life is meaningless without
a right relationship with Jesus Christ. Faith in Christ makes life
worthwhile. Our hopes, present, and future rest in Him.

Prayer

Lord, You are my light, my salvation, my present and future. You
are supreme in all that I do. Thank You for the peace, hope, and
joy that You give each day. Amen.

APRIL 26: PUT GOD FIRST

Remember God first, and honor
Him before the things of this earth!

In Ecclesiastes 12:1 (NLT), we read, "Don't let the excitement of youth cause you to forget your Creator. Honor Him in your youth before you grow old and say, 'Life is not pleasant anymore.'"

A life without God can produce bitterness, loneliness, and hopelessness in all ages. A life centered on God is fulfilling and rich, and it is more bearable when we are faced with disabilities, sickness, or handicaps. Being young is exciting, but it can become a barrier to closeness with God if young people choose to focus on pleasure instead of eternal values as they relate to God. Is God first in your life?

Prayer

Lord, teach me to seek You first in all that I do or say. Help me to put all my trust in You. Amen.

APRIL 27: FEAR GOD

Fear God by obeying and loving Him with all your heart!

In Ecclesiastes 12:13 (NLT), we read, "Here now is my final conclusion: Fear God and obey His commands, for this is everyone's duty."

Solomon knew God and was the wisest man of his day. He came to a profound conclusion that can be summed up in two parts: reverence God for who He is, and serve Him in an acceptable way based on His Word. Reverence and serve the Lord every chance you have.

Prayer

Lord, I reverence Your holy name. Teach me Your truth so that I will serve You with all my heart by precept and example. Amen.

_____
_____
_____
_____
_____
_____

APRIL 28: UNDONE

> I recognize that I'm undone, but I'm declared
> righteous by God's only Begotten Son!

Isaiah 6:5 (KJV) says, "Then said I, woe is me! For I am undone; because I am a man of unclean lips, and I dwell in the midst of a people of unclean lips: for mine eyes have seen the King, the Lord of Hosts."

When Isaiah saw God and heard the voice of the angels, he recognized his sins and the holiness of God. When we really get a glimpse of who God really is (through His Word and prayer), we too will see our sinfulness and confess our sins to Him.

Prayer

Lord, forgive me of all my sins, and cleanse me from all unrighteousness. Thank You for saving my soul. Amen.

APRIL 29: CHILD OF GOD

> To have Jesus as Savior, You must believe,
> so eternal life, you'll receive!

John 1:12 (NIV) says, "Yet to all who received Him, to those who believed in His name, He gave the right to become children of God."

Salvation is a choice. It is not automatic. God gives each person the right to become a child of God. However, each person must make the decision to receive the gift of new birth. Are you a child of God? Invite Jesus Christ into your heart, and He will save you.

Prayer

Lord Jesus, thank You for saving me. I am so grateful that Your Holy Spirit lives within and that You order my steps each day. Amen.

_____
_____
_____
_____
_____
_____

APRIL 30: USE YOUR GIFT

God has given you a gift, use it for others—to edify and lift.

Proverbs 18:16 (NIV) says, "A gift opens the way for the giver and ushers him into the presence of the great."

God has given each person something to offer that is unique. We must discover, develop, and utilize it to the glory of God, as we edify and help others. And by so doing, we open doors for blessing and promotion. What has God gifted you to do?

Prayer

Lord, teach me Your ways and show me how to use my gifts to glorify You. Then I will be able to serve and help others. Amen.

MAY

That at the name of Jesus every knee should bow, of things in heaven and things in earth, and things under the earth.
—Philippians 2:10 (NIV)

SAY THE NAME ...
JESUS

Justifier
Eternal Life Giver
Salvation Procurer
Unity Negotiator
Sanctifying Grace Provider

Shirley A. Howard

MAY 1: IN THE DAY OF TROUBLE

When trouble comes, I won't succumb but pray and trust,
Because Christ bled, died, and rose for us!

Psalm 50:15 (NIV) says, "And call upon me in the day of trouble;
I will deliver you, and you will honor me."

  When you know the goodness of God firsthand, your heart will
be filled with thanksgiving. You also know that there is nothing
that prayer can't fix. Prayer invites the Lord into our situation to
bless and strengthen us in whatever we are going through. Prayer
gives us a deeper understanding of God's power as we respond to
His love and faithfulness.

Prayer

Dear Lord, thank You for Your faithful love. I know that in this
life, we will have troubles, trials, and testing. But in all that I face,
I resolve to trust in You and not give up because I know You will
never give up on me. Amen.

MAY 2: GOD OUR REFUGE

> The Lord will guide and protect; trust and
> obey so your life, He will perfect!

Psalm 46:1 (NIV) says, "God is our refuge and strength, an everpresent help in trouble."

God is our shelter from dangers seen and unseen. Those who trust in the Lord find safety and courage because the Lord is always present to help in times of need.

Prayer

Lord, You shelter me from the storms of life. In You, there is no fear because You are with me continually. Thank You for Your faithfulness. Amen.

MAY 3: CAST IT ALL

Cast it all, God will catch you, lest you fall!

In 1 Peter 5:7 (NIV), we read, "Cast all your anxiety on Him because He cares for you."

The Lord knows what you are going through, and He is there with you in the midst of it all. Put all your trust in Him by casting all your concerns upon Jesus. By His mighty hand, He will sustain and comfort you. You must believe that God cares for you.

Prayer

Lord, come close so that I may feel Your tender care. Give me hope and strength for the journey each day. Please take away the pain and anxiety. This is my earnest prayer. Amen.

MAY 4: SECURE IN CHRIST

In Christ, the believer is secure. Her or his faith is made sure!

Psalm 125:1 (NIV) says, "Those who trust in the Lord are like Mount Zion, which cannot be shaken but endures forever."

Believers are secure, and they are unshakable because of their faith and trust in the Lord. Have you put all your trust in God?

Prayer

Lord, thank You for Your faithfulness. Though all around me changes, I have assurance that You will be there to steady my life's course. Amen.

MAY 5: DON'T WORRY

> Why worry when you can trust? For Christ
> died and rose again for us!

Matthew 6:31–32 (NIV) says, "So do not worry, saying, 'What shall we eat?' or 'What shall we drink?' or 'What shall we wear?' For the pagans run after all these things and your heavenly Father knows that you need them."

Jesus tells us not to worry about material things. Life is more important than these things. God has built into His creation the means by which all things are cared for. The birds of the air and the lilies of the field depend upon the Lord. Believers should be concerned first of all, about the things of God, His kingdom and His righteousness. When this happens, all these things will be supplied because the Lord knows what we need. He cares for us more than things.

Prayer

Thank You, Lord, that I don't have to worry about anything. Give me strength to do my part, as I trust You to provide for my needs. My hope and trust is in You. Amen.

_____

_____

_____

_____

_____

_____

MAY 6: SEEK THE LORD GOD

In all things, first seek God, and love Him with all your heart.

Matthew 6:33 (NIV) says, "But seek first His kingdom and His righteousness, and all these things will be given to you as well."

Seeking God first means to turn to Him first for help, to seek to be like Him in your thoughts, actions, and attitudes in daily life and as you relate to others. Putting God first is a choice each believer must make. The bottom line is that you must choose to put God first in all that you do. This extends to your relationship with others. Trust in Him, and do not doubt.

Prayer

Lord, thank You for Your faithful provision and love for me. Thank You for continually caring for me. Amen.

MAY 7: LEARN TO PLEASE GOD

God will provide for your needs, so trust and obey as He leads!

In Ecclesiastes 2:26 (NIV), we read, "To the man who pleases Him, God gives wisdom, knowledge, and happiness, but to the sinner, He gives the task of gathering and storing up wealth to hand it over to the one who pleases God. This too is meaningless, a chasing after the wind."

God will always provide for the needs of those who please Him. He gives wisdom, understanding, and joy to them. Those who please God live each day by faith and give thanks for His provisions. But those who do not obey God are on their own. They provide for their own needs rather than trusting God.

Prayer

Lord, my desire is to please You in all that I do. I rely on You to supply all that I need. Thank You for my daily provisions. Amen.

_____
_____
_____
_____
_____
_____

MAY 8: LET GOD TEACH

Let God teach you His way! He will guide
and keep you so you won't stray!

Psalm 32:8 (NIV) says, "I will instruct you and teach you in the way you should go; I will counsel you and watch over you."

God will teach us if we are willing to be taught. He desires to teach us step by step. He sees the paths that we take and wants to lead us with His love and wisdom.

Prayer

Lord, order my steps each day, I pray. Give me understanding so that I will seek You with all my heart. Amen.

MAY 9: SEEK HIS PATH

> Trust God's ways and seek His path; when you
> travel with Jesus, it's always first class!

Isaiah 2:3 (NIV) says, "Many people will come and say, 'Come let us go up to the mountain of the Lord, to the house of the God of Jacob. He will teach us His ways, so that we may walk in His paths. The law will go out from Zion, the word of the Lord from Jerusalem.'"

The ultimate fulfillment of this event will occur at a future time during the Millennium (one-thousand-year reign of Christ on earth). He will teach us His laws so that believers may obey His word. Those who belong to the Lord will enter into Zion, where Christ lives.

Prayer

Lord, thank You for Your faithfulness. Lead me in the path You have laid out for me. Teach me Your ways so that I will seek Your face. Amen.

_____
_____
_____
_____
_____
_____

MAY 10: BLESSED BY WHAT YOU READ, HEAR, AND DO

The Word of God is a blessing for those who read, hear, and do. It teaches them to trust in Jesus, who is the faithful and true!

Revelation 1:3 (NIV) says, "Blessed is the one who reads the words of this prophecy, and blessed are those who hear it and take to heart what is written in it, because the time is near."

God promises to bless each person who reads this book as well as the persons who hear it and accept its teaching. In other words, a reader will read this message aloud to an audience, and both will be blessed, especially those who respond in obedience. Faith comes by hearing and receiving the truth of God's Word. Today, the Word blesses us when read because it gives life and light and reveals God's truth.

Prayer

Thank You, Lord, for Your Holy Word. It is alive and powerful to all who believe. It brings comfort and peace and gives rest to those in need. Thank You for all that You give. Amen.

MAY 11: GOD'S WORD IS LIGHT

God's Word is the light that shines bright,
bringing forth spiritual insight!

Psalm 119:130 (NIV) says, "The unfolding of your words gives light; it gives understanding to the simple."

The Word of God unfolds and exposes the character and nature of Holy God. It is the light that dispels the darkness of our souls, giving understanding to those who were once without it.

Prayer

Lord, You give me light through Your Holy Word. Thank You for providing wisdom to understand Your truths. Amen.

_____
_____
_____
_____
_____
_____

MAY 12: GOD'S WORD IS TRUE WISDOM

God's Holy Word contains the wisdom that you seek. Those
who follow it become powerful, humble, and meek!

In 2 Timothy 3:15–16 (NIV), we read, "And how from infancy
you have known the Holy Scriptures, which are able to make you
wise for salvation through faith in Christ Jesus. All Scripture is
Godbreathed and is useful for teaching, rebuking, correcting and
training in righteousness."

Paul charges Timothy to hold to what is in him. The Word
was taught to him by his mother and grandmother when he was a
small child. Paul encouraged Timothy to develop his faith and grow
continually by teaching and preaching the Word to others. We are
encouraged to pass on the legacy of Holy Scripture to our children.
The Bible is more than stories about God; it is God-breathed. This
means that God inspired people over the ages, by the Holy Spirit,
to write down His words for humanity. His Word is completely
trustworthy and powerful to save and heal. Share with others what
you know about Jesus, and you too will grow spiritually.

Prayer

All-wise, mighty, and living God, stir up the gift You have placed
in me. Show me my purpose so that I will do Your holy will, Your
way. Amen.

MAY 13: FAITH IN THE WORD OF GOD

> By faith in the Word, God's voice is heard, and
> His strength and power undergird!

Romans 10:17 (NIV) says, "Consequently, faith comes from hearing the message, and the message is heard through the Word of Christ."

The Word of God can only be received by faith. To hear means to respond with a positive response—to obey and submit to the Lord. Hearing (responding to) the message of Jesus Christ is what saves. He calls us to hear His message of love and receive it by living by it.

Prayer

Thank You for Your Word and its ability to awaken my spirit to hear Your Spirit speak to my heart. I am renewed every day. Thank You, Jesus; thank You, Holy Spirit; and thank You, Father God. Amen.

_____
_____
_____
_____
_____
_____

MAY 14: A HEART AND MIND FOR GOD

> Give God your heart; give Him your mind;
> entrust your whole life to the Divine!

Deuteronomy 11:18 (NIV) says, "Fix these words of mine in your hearts and minds, tie them as symbols on your hands and bind them on your foreheads."

Israel was prone to stray away from God (as we are) and was easily enticed by pagan gods. God informed His people to remember His words by hiding them in their hearts. In other words, they had to make a conscious decision (as we do) to trust and obey God's commands. We are faced with temptations daily, and we must choose to follow Jesus.

Prayer

Lord, thank You that my mind is stayed on You. Thank You for giving me a heart that seeks to obey Your will and way. And in the tough times when I'm tempted to give up, let me sense Your presence and power near me. Amen.

_____
_____
_____
_____
_____
_____

MAY 15: COMMIT TO GOD

> Commit to God first; in Jesus, we have second
> birth. He came to save the people of earth!

Acts 20:32 (NIV) reads, "Now I commit you to God and to the word of His grace, which can build you up and give you an inheritance among all those who are sanctified."

As we commit to the Word of His grace, it is done only by faith through obedience to His Word. This will lead to your edification (building up) and to an inheritance with Jesus. Truth (God's Word) and obedience go hand and hand. We trust God's Word by obeying it. Obedience leads to righteousness.

Prayer

Lord, thank You for Your provision and faithfulness. It is Your Word that builds me up and sets me on a solid footing. I give my whole being to You. All that I am and ever will be rests in You. Teach me Your Truth (Word). Amen.

_____
_____
_____
_____
_____
_____

MAY 16: WHAT GOD SPEAKS COMES TO PASS

When God speaks a thing, it will come to pass.
Only what you do for Him will last!

Isaiah 55:11 (NIV) says, "So is my word that goes out from my mouth: It will not return to me empty, but will accomplish what I desire and achieve the purpose for which I sent it."

Just as the rain and snow fall down to the earth, quenching its thirst, so is God's Word that comes from His mouth bringing refreshment to the soul. What God says will truly come to pass. His Word can be trusted, and by faith, it becomes a reality in our lives through the power of the Holy Spirit. Believe and trust God today!

Prayer

Lord, thank You for Your Word, for it is true and dependable. You cannot lie. I praise Your holy name. Amen.

MAY 17: REMAIN IN HIM

As we remain in Christ, He remains in us and
answers our prayers when we faithfully trust!

John 15:7 (NIV) says, "If you remain in me and my words remain
in you, ask whatever you wish, and it will be given you."

Prayer is based on faith in Jesus Christ and according to His
Word that is at work in us. His Word changes us by giving us
His mind and heart, and it conforms us to His image. By faith,
our will becomes His will, and our prayers are answered. When
we have His heart and mind, what we ask for in prayer is what
He desires; therefore, we receive what we ask for because it is His
desire to give it.

Prayer

Lord, I thank You for Your Word within my heart, which is
transforming my will into Your will, so that my prayers will be
answered according to Your purpose. I love You, Lord. Amen.

MAY 18: CHOSEN BY THE LORD

Lord, I'm chosen by You, so that I'm assured
that all I face, You'll guide me through!

John 15:16 (NIV) says, "You did not choose me, but I chose you and appointed you to go and bear fruit—fruit that will last. Then the Father will give you whatever you ask in my name."

We are blessed to know that Jesus chose us first. Then He appointed us to bear fruit. This assures us that He has given us what we need to be fruitful. And if we have any lack, all we need to do is ask the Father in Jesus's name. Christ chose us, thus giving us a choice to accept His offer of love and salvation. Choose to follow Jesus.

Prayer

Dear Lord, thank You for choosing me. You reached out to me and gave me a choice to become Your own. And You put in me the ability to succeed. Thank You for giving me a choice to choose Your love and grace. Amen.

MAY 19: BIND AND LOOSE

You give us power to bind and loose things on earth!
This privilege comes with the new birth!

Matthew 18:18 (NIV) says, "I tell you the truth, whatever you bind on earth will be bound in heaven, and whatever you loose on earth will be loosed in heaven."

Jesus was speaking specifically about disputes or disagreements in the church among members. Whatever is bound or loosed should be based on God-centered principles outlined in the Word of God. So whatever we do or say should be rooted in the truth of God's Word.

Prayer

Lord, I thank You that You have given me the authority and ability to make right decisions based on Your Holy Word. You are always there to guide me when I ask. Amen.

MAY 20: APPROACH GOD WITH CONFIDENCE

With confidence, we boldly come into Your holy place,
where we graciously receive your power and grace!

In 1 John 5:14–15 (NIV), we read, "This is the confidence we
have in approaching God: that if we ask anything according to His
will, He hears us. And if we know that He hears us—whatever we
ask—we know that we have what we asked of Him."

The emphasis is not on what we want or desire; it is on God's
will. We have the privilege to present our petition or case to the
Lord, but He has the final say. As our will becomes aligned with
His will, we receive the petition that we ask for from the Lord.
Do you seek God's will?

Prayer

Thank You for hearing my prayers and giving me the privilege
to come boldly into Your holy presence in prayer. You teach me
to know Your heart and will for my life and how to intercede for
myself and others. Thank You, my Lord, for all that You do. Amen.

MAY 21: NOTHING IS IMPOSSIBLE WITH GOD

We serve the God who does impossible things—
peace, joy, provision, and protection He brings!

Mark 9:23 (NIV) says, "If you can, said Jesus, Everything is possible for Him who believes."

These words do not mean that we will automatically receive everything we want if we think positively about it. Anything is possible if we believe in Jesus. There is nothing too hard for God. By faith (when we pray) we can have everything we need to serve Him. We have the privilege to ask for what we need from the Lord because we belong to Him. He delights in answering prayers, yet God has the final say.

Prayer

Lord, I come boldly to You in prayer, believing that You can do anything but fail. You have all power, and all things are under Your control. Thank You for being my mighty God and my strong, high tower. I love and adore You. Amen.

MAY 22: FAITH VERSUS DOUBT

Faith says, "Yes, I can!"
Doubt says, "I don't know God's plan; therefore,
I don't truly trust His holy hands.

Matthew 21:21–22 (NIV) says, "Jesus replied, 'I tell you the truth, if you have faith and do not doubt, not only can you do what was done to the fig tree [vv. 18–19], but also you can say to this mountain, go throw yourself into the sea, and it will be done. If you believe, you will receive whatever you ask in prayer."

The emphasis is on faith, not on magical formulas. Faith without doubting draws us closer to the revelation of God's power. As we draw closer to Him by faith, we better understand His will and purpose for our lives. What mountains are you facing? Do you believe that God can do all that He says?

Prayer

Lord, increase my faith and understanding of who You are. Help me recognize and utilize the measure of faith You have given me. May I know the joy of trusting You without doubting. Amen.

MAY 23: GOD'S WAY

I seek to live Your way
—to study and obey Your Word every day!

Isaiah 55:9 (NIV) says, "As the heavens are higher than the earth, so are my ways higher than your ways and my thoughts than your thoughts."

God's knowledge and wisdom are superior to all others. His ways are far removed from ours. We cannot begin to know the deep ways and thoughts of God unless He chooses to reveal Himself to us by the Holy Spirit and through His Word.

Prayer

Lord, thank You for Your wisdom and knowledge, which surpasses all human understanding. Help me to always conform to Your will and way rather than seek my own. Teach me to live within Your will. Amen.

MAY 24: GOD IS NOT SLOW

The Lord is not slow;
rather He patiently allows time
for us to grow!

In 2 Peter 3:9 (NIV), we read, "The Lord is not slow in keeping His promises as some understand slowness. He is patient with you, not wanting anyone to perish, but everyone to come to repentance."

The Lord is not slow, though it seems at times that He is. He is not on our timetable, and His goals and objectives are far different from ours. He is not limited by time; rather He operates within time and eternity to accomplish His purposes. God is patient as He waits for the unsaved to repent. Believers are part of God's plan to save others by sharing the gospel with them. Have you shared the gospel with a family member, friend, or acquaintance today?

Prayer

Lord, teach me to patiently wait on You. Align my will with Your work as You reveal to me what my assignment is on earth. Thank You for saving me; give me courage so that I will help save others. Amen.

_____
_____
_____
_____
_____
_____

MAY 25: HE DIED IN OUR PLACE

> Christ died in our place, giving us power to be saved and
> run this Christian race by His strength and grace!

In 1 Peter 2:24 (NIV), we read, "He Himself bore our sins in his body on the tree, so that we might die to sins and live for righteousness; by his wounds you have been healed."

Christ died in our place. He took away the penalty and power of sin over us. Because He died in our place, we can claim His righteousness and have power to do good and shun evil. He was wounded so that we may be healed. We are healed so that we may bear witness to others of Christ's healing power.

Prayer

Thank You, Jesus, for dying in my place and giving me eternal life. I now have the power to resist sin and live a life of victory. It is by Your wounds that I am made whole in Jesus's name. Amen.

_____
_____
_____
_____
_____
_____

MAY 26: GOD SUPPLIES ALL

> Trust and believe that God supplies all. Obey; then
> you'll know that He will catch you so you don't
> fall and will attend to your faintest call!

Philippians 4:19 (NIV) says, "And my God will meet all your needs according to His glorious riches in Christ Jesus."

We can trust that the Lord will supply all our needs but not necessarily all our wants. He supplies our needs according to His purpose. We are not exempt from trials and suffering in life. We are assured by the Bible that He will never leave us alone. Also, as we supply the needs of others, the Lord will supply our needs when we trust Him. It is through the redemptive work of Christ that all our needs are supplied.

Prayer

Lord, I know You will supply my every need. I thank You for Your kind care and daily provisions. Amen.

_____
_____
_____
_____
_____
_____

MAY 27: IN THE GAP

> Christ stood in the gap so sin, death, and
> the grave, He would eternally zap!

Matthew 8:17 (NIV) says, "This was to fulfill what was spoken through the Prophet Isaiah: 'He took up our infirmities and carried our diseases.'"

Jesus touched people, and they were healed; He spoke and demons came out of people. Jesus has control over all sickness and disease; He is able to rid the world of sin and death. Jesus has the same power today, and He commands us to believe and not doubt." His plan is to enlist believers to share the gospel with the world.

Prayer

Lord Jesus, thank You for being my Savior and Lord. I know You control all things. Touch my body, I pray, so that I will be physically and spiritually whole. And of your goodness, I will share with others. Amen.

_____
_____
_____
_____
_____
_____

MAY 28: JESUS IS THE LIGHT

Jesus is the True Light, who reveals light. So come
out of darkness, and do what is right!

John 12:46 (NIV) says, "I have come into the world as a light, so
that no one who believes in me should stay in darkness."

Jesus came to lead people out of Satan's kingdom of darkness
into God's eternal kingdom of light and love. Because He came
from the Father, Christ is the Light of the world. Believers choose
to walk in His light and are commissioned to share the light with
those who are in the dark.

Prayer

Jesus, You are the Light of the world, and in You, there is no darkness
or evil at all. Thank You for saving me and depositing the light of
Your Spirit in my heart. Amen.

_____
_____
_____
_____
_____
_____

MAY 29: BELIEVE AND THEN RECEIVE

Believe God's Word, and you will receive—to
receive is the result of what you believe!

Mark 11:24 (NIV) says, "Therefore, I tell you, whatever you ask for in prayer, believe that you have received it, and it will be your."

Believing prayer taps into the power of God in order to do the humanly impossible. The Lord invites us to believe that we have already received what we asked for in prayer, even though we don't have it currently. True faith considers a thing already done in Jesus's name.

Prayer

Almighty God, there is nothing You cannot do. Increase my faith to know that You will do the humanly impossible in my life. Heal my body, and give me strength to endure. In Jesus's name, I pray. Amen.

MAY 30: CHIEF CORNERSTONE

> Christ is the chief cornerstone. He supports and upholds
> us with assurance that we are never alone!

In 1 Peter 2:6 (NIV), we read, "For in Scripture it says: 'see I lay a stone in Zion, a chosen and precious cornerstone, and the one who trusts in Him will never be put to shame."

Jesus is the stone in Zion. He is chosen and precious. He is also our cornerstone—giving strength and stability as we put our faith and trust in Him. We trust and rely on Him, knowing that we will never be ashamed. He won't give up on us, and He offers victory to those who persevere in their faith.

Prayer

Lord, You are my sturdy and sure foundation. All my help and support comes from You. You keep and sustain me in times of trouble. Thank You, Lord, that I won't be put to shame. Amen.

MAY 31: THE BREAD OF LIFE

> Jesus is the living bread that gives eternal life—
> it was wrought at a great price!

John 6:35 (NIV) says, "Then Jesus declared, 'I am the bread of life. He who comes to me will never go hungry, and he who believes in me will never be thirsty.'"

Just as physical bread feeds the physically hungry and sustains life, so Jesus is the bread of life that satisfies the spiritual life. And as a cool drink of water quenches the physically thirsty, likewise the living water refreshes a thirsty soul. Jesus is the living spiritual bread, and the Holy Spirit is the living water that provides sustained nourishment and uplifts both body and soul.

Prayer

Father, sustain me with Your living bread. Jesus is the living bread. Feed me until I want no more. Take my spiritual cup, fill it up, and let it overflow with Your goodness. In Jesus's name, I pray. Amen.

JUNE

The wilderness and the solitary place shall be glad for them;
and the desert shall rejoice, and blossom like the rose.
—Isaiah 35:1 (NIV)

A ROSE

A beautiful red rose—
Slowly, slowly, it grows.
Its velvety softness
Embraces the nose,
And its fragrance goes
Forth for all to behold!
Shirley A. Howard

Let your life be as fragrant as a rose.

JUNE 1: NEVER GIVE UP

> Don't you quit, for deep within your soul,
> God's Holy Ghost fire is lit!

Luke 18:1 (NIV) says, "Then Jesus told His disciples a parable to show them that they should always pray and not give up."

Whatever you pray for, do not give up, but keep praying until God gives you an answer. Blessings come to those who do not give up but press on.

Prayer

Lord, thank You for hearing my prayer today. Help me not to give up when things do not go the way that I expect. I love you, and I refuse to give up. Amen.

_____
_____
_____
_____
_____
_____

JUNE 2: CALL WHEN DISTRESSED

When you become distressed, recognize that it may be
a test; for the Lord desires to bring out your best.

Psalm 18:6 (NIV) says, "In my distress I called to the Lord, I cried
to my God for help. From His temple He heard my voice; my cry
comes before Him into His ears."

David expressed the assurance that God hears his cry for help,
and from His holy temple, God comes to rescue him. We can have
the same blessed assurance today when we cry out to the Lord.
He loves, hears, and delivers His own. He calls us to trust in Him
when things seem hopeless.

Prayer

Thank You, Lord, for hearing my prayers and coming to my aid
at just the right moment in time. You hear and act on my behalf.
I am so grateful for Your faithfulness. Amen.

_____
_____
_____
_____
_____
_____

JUNE 3: GOD KNOWS

The way I go, God knows, and His faithfulness to me shows!
His love is more precious than pure gold!

Job 23:10 (NIV) says, "But He knows the way that I take; when He has tested me, I will come forth as gold."

We can rest in the fact that the Lord knows all about us. He sees every minute detail in every life. He guides and protects our paths and works to move us to a desired end!

Prayer

Lord, I thank you that I have hope. Everywhere I go, You are there guiding and protecting, as you bring out the best in me today. Amen.

_____
_____
_____
_____
_____

JUNE 4: FIGHT GOOD

> I fight the good fight, as my God holds me
> tight and will make things right!

In 1 Timothy 6:12 (NIV), we read, "Fight the good fight of faith. Take hold of the eternal life to which you were called when you made your good confession in the presence of many witnesses."

Now is the time for us to believe God and trust His Word. There are times when we must stand our ground and not quit—even if it appears that we're going down for the count. Don't quit, because we are "more than conquerors" (Romans 8:37). God will cause us to be victorious if we believe His Word and do not give up.

Prayer

Mighty God and Everlasting Father, give me strength and Your power to stay in the fight of faith today. Though I may lose a round or two, the battle is Yours, and I won't quit, for the victory is mine. In Jesus's name, I pray. Amen.

_____
_____
_____
_____
_____
_____

JUNE 5: YOU ARE SALT

Jesus said that you are salt. Are you living each day as you ought, by obeying and sharing what the Master taught?

Matthew 5:13 (NIV) says, "You are the salt of the earth. But if the salt loses its saltiness, how can it be made salty again? It is no longer good for anything except to be thrown out and trampled by men."

Jesus described us as being salt in this world. Salt was used to do several things: make you thirsty, preserve things, and make food taste better. As salt of the earth, we can make people thirsty to know God and help build faith to preserve against the evil of society by sharing the Word of God, and we can be savory by cultivating and showing the love of Jesus to others.

Prayer

Lord, please don't allow me to lose my spiritual saltiness. May I continually thirst for a clearer understanding of Your Word as I tell others of Your goodness and love today. Strengthen me when I feel weak and weary. Bless me now, so that I may be a blessing to my family and others. Amen.

JUNE 6: WAIT WITH PATIENCE

When you are still,
God is there waiting
your soul and spirit to fill!

Psalm 37:7 (NIV) says, "Be still before the Lord and wait patiently for Him."

Faith requires waiting patiently for the Lord to answer. When our prayer is not answered immediately, faith does not give up; it waits on God to answer. God sometimes uses delays to test our faith so we may grow as He desires.

Prayer

Lord, quieten my heart before You today. Help me to patiently wait on You. You know all things, and You do all things well. Only You can fill my greatest expectations in this life. Amen.

JUNE 7: GOD PRESERVES

> God will keep us and preserve us—by His grace; He
> never gives us the judgment that we deserve!

Psalm 16:1 (NIV) says, "Keep me safe, O God, for in you I take refuge."

This psalm of David discusses how he came to know and trust the Lord. This verse is a summary of the entire psalm. The Lord keeps us safe and secure as we learn to trust Him with all our hearts. Are you trusting Him today?

Prayer

Lord, keep me in the center of Your will. Keep Your loving arms around me, and protect me from dangers seen and unseen. Preserve my way so that I may lead others into your perfect way. Amen.

_____
_____
_____
_____
_____
_____

JUNE 8: YOU KNOW MY PATH

> Lord, You control the path of my life. In Your
> Word, You give sound advice—
> I have total trust in Jesus Christ!

Psalm 16:11 (NIV) says, "You have made known to me the path of life; You will fill me with joy in Your presence, with eternal pleasures at Your right hand."

David expresses confidence in God's provision and protection. His faith is made sure in the Lord. God knows David, and David knows the Lord; therefore, his heart was filled with joy. David is assured that he has eternal life in God's presence. The Lord desires for us to have the same assurance. Are you secure in your faith and trust of Him?

Prayer

You are my Lord, and You provide all my needs. Without You, I can do nothing. I trust You to see me through all that I face each day. Thank You for loving me. Amen.

_____
_____
_____
_____
_____
_____

JUNE 9: MY STRENGTH

Jesus is the strength of my life, and I love Him because (just for me) He was willing to pay sin's price!

Psalm 18:1 (NIV) says, "I love You, O Lord, my Strength."

Like the psalmist says, the Word of God brings joy to the heart when we reflect upon God's awesome greatness and all that He has done for us.

Prayer

Lord, You are my high tower when all my strength is gone. Your love teaches and gives me reasons to love You more deeply day by day. I love You, Lord, with all my heart. Amen.

JUNE 10: GOD IS ALL I NEED

> All I need, my God will provide! With His mighty
> hand of power, He leads and guides!

Psalm 18:2 (NIV) says, "The Lord is my rock, my fortress and my deliverer; my God is my rock, in whom I take refuge. He is my shield and the horn of my salvation, my stronghold."

Like David, we too discover, in times of trouble, that God will be there as a rock to provide stability. And when we trust Him, He becomes a fortress of refuge and a defense of protection in whatever we go through.

Prayer

Lord, thank You for being everything that I need—my Protector, my Shield, my Stronghold, and the Author and Finisher of my Salvation. Keep me from being afraid of the challenges I may face on this day. Amen.

JUNE 11: HE HEARS WHEN I CALL

> When I call, God hears; when I trust and
> not doubt, He calms all my fears!

Psalm 18:3 (NIV) says, "I call to the Lord, who is worthy of praise, and I am saved from my enemies."

Again, David acknowledges that because the Lord is all he needs, God is worthy of all praise. In the Lord, we too can find safety and provision from all that we face each day.

Prayer

Lord, I praise You for who You are. And I'm so grateful for all that You have done and will do. Thank You for your continued faithfulness to me. Amen.

JUNE 12: HOW LONG, O LORD?

> I ask, "How long, O Lord, how long?"
> I hear the Spirit say, "Not long!
> For soon your trouble will be gone!"

Psalm 13:4–6 (NIV) says, "But I trust in Your unfailing love; my heart rejoices in Your salvation. I will sing to the Lord for He has been good to me."

Waiting sometimes causes us to become weary and discouraged. But we must resolve in our spirit to trust in the Lord's unfailing love. We must wait until our change comes and let Him give us a new song of rejoicing. Never doubt God's love and faithfulness.

Prayer

Lord, I wait patiently on You to move on my behalf. My heart fills with joy as You put a new song of praise and thanksgiving in my heart. I delight in Your steadfast love. Thank You for Your goodness toward me today. Amen.

JUNE 13: GOD'S COMPASSION

God's compassion is new every day. He ever
provides and makes a way as we daily pray!

Lamentations 3:23–24 (NIV) says, "They (God's compassions)
are new every morning; great is Your faithfulness. I say to myself,
the Lord is my portion; therefore I will wait for Him."

We are able to stand because God's compassions never fail. At
times, we may be down, but we are not out; His loyal love holds us
fast and draws us to the cross of Christ. He is faithful and provides
what we need. So we wait confidently on Him to move because
of His great love for us.

Prayer

Thank You, Lord, for Your great love and faithfulness to me no
matter what situation I'm in. I trust You to always be there to
help me in times of need. Allow me to experience Your presence
throughout this day. Amen.

JUNE 14: A CAUSE TO PRAISE

Lord, You give us a genuine heart to praise Your name.
At Calvary,
Jesus bore the shame so that eternal life and joy we claim!

Psalm 150:2 (NIV) says, "Praise Him for His acts of power; praise Him for His surpassing greatness."

There is always a reason to praise God. He is the Maker and Creator of everything. He set order in this vast universe and everything in it. We praise Him for His mighty excellence seen in the things that He does. His voice speaks to us in the deep silence of the heart. And He stills our countenance and calms our fears.

Prayer

Lord, I worship and praise You for who You are. You are the all-powerful God, and there is no one greater than You. Thank You for keeping me today and all the days of my life. Amen.

JUNE 15: ALL CREATION GIVES PRAISE

Let all of creation give the Lord praise all their days!

Psalm 150:6 (NIV) says, "Let everything that has breath praise the Lord. Praise the Lord."

This is a call for every living thing that has breath in it to give praise to the Lord our God with its whole being. There is no god like our God, who rides the winds, who directs the sun and moon, and who orchestrates the stars in the sky. Oh, how marvelous is our God!

Prayer

Lord, I thank You for life, and I praise You for who you are. There is nothing that You have not made. You are Maker and Sustainer of everything. So I am confident that You will keep me throughout this day. Amen.

_____

_____

_____

_____

_____

JUNE 16: KNOWING CHRIST IS PRIORITY ONE

Lord, my goal in life is to know You. For Your
will and way are tried and true!

Philippians 3:8 (NIV) says, "Yes, everything else is worthless when compared with the infinite value of knowing Christ Jesus, my Lord. For His sake, I have discarded everything else, counting it all as garbage, so that I could gain Christ."

When Paul observed all the things he had done in his life, he concluded that it was worthless when compared to knowing Jesus. To know Christ is the most important and necessary thing in life. You begin to know Christ by the study of His Word, through worship, praise, thanksgiving, and prayer as you live out the precepts of His truth. The Holy Spirit lives inside to teach us how to know and please God.

Prayer

Lord, I want to know You in Your fullness. To know You is my ultimate goal in this life. Teach and show me Your truth, for Your Word is truth. In all that I go through, draw me closer to You each and every day. Amen.

JUNE 17: PRAISE FOR UNDERSTANDING

God will teach you to understand as you seek to know His holy plan!

Psalm 119:12 (NIV) says, "I praise You, O Lord; teach me your decrees!"

The psalmist recognized the greatness of His God, as he expressed his heartfelt praise and thanksgiving with a desire to understand God's laws more fully. Just as he asked God to teach him, we too can ask the Lord to give us a deeper revelation of who He is. The Lord desires for us to know Him more intimately.

Prayer

O Lord, You are worthy of all praise. Thank You for giving me a clearer understanding of Your purpose for my life. Help me to see clearly Your overall plan; then give me wisdom and strength to live it each day. Amen.

_____
_____
_____
_____
_____
_____

JUNE 18: STUDY HIS COMMANDS

I study Your commands, observing your demands—
knowing full well that Your hand is holding my hand!

Psalm 119:15 (NIV) says, "I will study your commands and reflect
on your ways."

Many view the commands of the Lord as being restrictive. As
you study the Word, you will discover that God's laws were given
to free us to be all He wants us to be. His Word helps us follow
His path and avoid paths that lead to destruction.

Prayer

Lord, guide my steps in Your Word, and lead me in the right paths
that draw me closer to You. Continue to love and walk with me,
and draw me closer to You through meditation on Your Word in
prayer. Thank You for Your faithfulness to me and my family. Amen.

JUNE 19: HE HEARS YOUR FAITHFUL CRY

Have no fear, for Your God is near.
He loves you and holds you dear!
He will come alongside and wipe away each tear!

Psalm 27:7 (NIV) says, "Hear my voice when I call, O Lord; be merciful to me and answer me."

David is the writer of this psalm. We often seek after God when we are faced with difficulties. But the Lord delights in us when we seek guidance and not just when there is a problem. He gives us the ability to solve any problem that may arise as we get to know Him more intimately. Do you have an earnest desire to know God?

Prayer

Lord, hear my prayer. Be merciful to me in times of distress, for I delight in spending time with You each day. Draw near to me and answer my prayer as You desire. Let Your grace and mercy be on my left and right sides as I cry out to You. Thank You for hearing my prayers. Amen.

_____
_____
_____
_____
_____
_____

JUNE 20: EARNEST PRAYER IN FAITH

By faith, earnestly seek Your God, for He will
answer in His time if you do not lose heart!

Psalm 27:8 (NIV) says, "My heart says of you, 'Seek his face!' Your
face, Lord, I will seek."

The Lord may not answer at the time you want Him to answer,
but God will answer. By faith, earnestly seek Him with your whole
heart. Trust the Lord even when you do not understand what He is
doing. Trust the Lord to always do what is right and just concerning
your present and future. In your spirit, chase after the Lord with
your whole being. Do not relent until the answer from God is sent!

Prayer

O Lord, my heart and soul long to hear from You. I seek Your
guidance, protection, and provision right now. Come, sweet Jesus,
and deliver me from hurt, harm, and danger. Draw me closer today,
in Jesus's name. Amen.

JUNE 21: GIVE THANKS TO GOD

Give thanks to God; open up your heart as
you keep your gaze heavenward!

In 1 Chronicles 16:8 (NIV), we read, "Give thanks to the Lord, call
on his name; make known among the nations what He has done."

This is a reminder of the joy released in our souls as we
contemplate the goodness of God. This verse reminds us why we
should be thankful and find joy in the privilege to call on His name
in prayer. His goodness is so overwhelming that we can't keep it
to ourselves. If the Lord has done something for you, you must
tell someone—anyone!

Prayer

O my Lord, I thank You because there is no one like You. I love
to call Your name and share Your goodness with everyone I meet.
Thanksgiving and praise break forth out of my mouth when I
contemplate the wonders of who You are. Thank You for the privilege
to serve and proclaim Your name to all who will hear. Amen.

_____
_____
_____
_____
_____
_____

JUNE 22: LOOK TO THE LORD

Look to Him; seek His face;
The enemy can't condemn when you're wrapped in His grace!

In 1 Chronicles 16:11 (NIV), we read, "Look to the Lord and his strength; seek his face always."

We find victory when we put our focus on the Lord. He abides within and strengthens us to always seek His precepts and values in our daily life.

Prayer

My faith and confidence rests in You, O Lord. As You continue to abide within my heart, I am strengthened by Your power and grace. I will seek Your face in all I do today! I lift up holy hands in prayer with a grateful heart strengthened and kept by You. Amen.

_____
_____
_____
_____
_____
_____

JUNE 23—LORD, I REMEMBER YOU

> Lord, I remember You, and each wonder and miracle You
> brought me through—Your grace and mercy, I pursue!

In 1 Chronicles 16:12 (NIV), we read, "Remember the wonders
he has done, his miracles, and the judgments he pronounced."

It is a blessing from the Lord to reflect upon the wonders
and miracles that He wrought in our lives. We must never forget
what the Lord brings us through and the judgments on those who
oppose His will and way.

Prayer

Thank You, Lord, for all Your benefits and the wonders and
miracles that You perform before my eyes each day. My heart and
soul are focused continually on You. I trust and rely on Your grace
and mercy to lead and guide me day by day. For I know that Your
judgments are righteous and true. Amen.

_____

_____

_____

_____

_____

_____

JUNE 24: WHAT CAN HE NOT DO?

There is nothing God can't do, when by faith
in His Holy Word, you remain true!

Genesis 18:14 (NIV) says, "Is anything too hard for the Lord?"

God asked Sarah this question. Each of us must by faith answer it for ourselves. We must not doubt what the Lord can do. In order to survive and thrive, we must know deep within our heart and soul that there is nothing too hard for our God.

Prayer

Thank You, Lord, that I am assured of Your power and ability. I know that You are able to do all things, and do them perfectly. I invite You to take charge of my life because You are the one true God, and besides You, there is no other. Amen.

JUNE 25: FAITH AND HOPE

Faith in God will carry you, and hope will keep
and sustain you on your life journey!

Genesis 49:18 (NIV) says, "I look for your deliverance, O Lord."

Never give up on God. Always trust in His Word, hope in Him, and rest in His promises.

Prayer

Lord, I believe in You, and I trust in You with my whole heart. Each day, I wait patiently on You to speak to my heart and guide my ways. I wait for Your goodness to unfold me as You deliver me and loved ones from harm. Amen.

JUNE 26: WARRIOR GOD

My cause, You will defend—so totally on You I depend!

Exodus 15:3 (NIV) says, "The Lord is a Warrior; the Lord is his name."

Moses acknowledged the strength and might of God when He destroyed the Egyptian army in the Red Sea. God's strength and power to defend is available to us today. What enemies are you facing?

Prayer

Lord, I know You to be a Mighty Warrior who will fight for me in times of trouble. Come to my aid today in all that I must face. I totally trust in You alone. I cast all my cares upon You. Amen.

JUNE 27: NO ONE LIKE YOU, LORD

Your glory and splendor reign supreme. We take joy in knowing that by Christ's blood, we've been redeemed!

Exodus 15:11 (NIV) says, "Who among the gods is like you, O Lord? Who is like you—majestic in holiness, awesome in glory, working wonders?"

When we begin to see clearly and experience the power and majesty of God, like Moses, we will praise Him too. As we spend time with the Lord in study and meditative prayer, He reveals to us how mighty and awesome He is.

Prayer

Thank You, Lord, for Your mighty power. I know firsthand that there is no other god like You. Allow Your holy presence to manifest Your power and goodness in my life today. Amen.

JUNE 28: TO LOVE GOD IS TO OBEY GOD

You measure my love for You by how well I obey.
You are faithful to show me how to live Your way!

Deuteronomy 11:1 (NIV) says, "Love the Lord your God and keep his requirements, his decrees, his laws and commands always."

Do you love the Lord? Throughout scripture, the test of a believer's love for God is based on his or her obedience to His Holy Word. Do you trust and obey Him?

Prayer

Lord, thank You for Your grace, faithfulness, and love, which you extend to me even when I don't obey Your commands. Keep me on the right path today and every day, I pray. Amen.

JUNE 29: WHO IS YOUR ROCK?

Jesus is the Rock. Trust Him and obey, and you'll
experience His peace and protection around the clock!

Deuteronomy 32:4 (NIV) declares, "He is the Rock, His works
are perfect, and all His ways are just. A faithful God who does no
wrong, upright and just is he."

The Lord is our Rock. He is strong and mighty, and He is the
only stability that we have in life. By clinging to Him, we are kept
safe and secure from the enemy's snares.

Prayer

Lord, You are the strength of my life, and all my help comes from
You. You are holy and just, faithful and true to Your Words. Guide
me through this day and protect me from the obstacles that seek
to block my way. These things I ask in Jesus's name. Amen.

JUNE 30: GREAT IS OUR GOD

> Great is our God, no force on earth or above can
> separate us from His protection and love!

In 2 Samuel 22:3 (NIV), we read, "My God is my Rock in whom I take refuge; my shield and the horn of my salvation. He is my stronghold, my refuge and my savior—from violent men, you save me."

David acknowledged the greatness and glory of God with a series of words that described his feelings and thoughts as he was pursued by King Saul. Throughout David's life, the Lord had been these things to him. What has the Lord been for you? Take time to reflect and give Him praise and thanks.

Prayer

Lord, thank You that I can declare all the marvelous things You are to me. You are my life, the very breath that I breathe. You are my everything. There is nobody like You, Jesus. You commune with me each day. Thank You for Your faithfulness and for being my friend. Amen.

JULY

Keep me as the apple of the eye; hide me
under the shadow of thy wings.
—Psalm 17:8 (KJV)

BUTTERFLY

Butterfly, butterfly, don't you stop;
Just continue to fly to and fro in
The sky!

Don't stop, for you can go high—
And higher if you give it a try!

Your beauty is seen everywhere
You go! Passersby stop or they
Slow just to see your beauty!

Butterfly, continue to fly, fluttering
Your wings as you go, doing what
Your Creator designed you to do!

Keep on going, and His desired
Destiny He'll lead you to!

Butterfly, butterfly, don't you stop;
Just continue to fly purposely
Through the open sky!

Shirley A. Howard

JULY 1: STRONG FAITH AND OVERFLOWING THANKSGIVING

A strong faith and overflowing thanksgiving
in Jesus will result in thanks-living!

Colossians 2:6–7 (NIV) says, "So then, just as you received Christ Jesus as Lord, continue to live in Him, rooted and built up in Him, strengthened in the faith as you were taught, and overflowing with thanksgiving."

Receiving Christ in your life is the beginning of eternal and abundant life with Him. You accomplish this through prayer, the study of His Word, and obeying the Word. These things build up faith and help us to stay rooted in Christ. As we grow in our knowledge of Christ, our heart is filled with His love and gratitude that produces overflowing thanksgiving. The indwelling Holy Spirit guides and directs us in daily living.

Prayer

Lord, thank You for saving my soul and for the indwelling Holy Spirit to lead and guide me each day. I delight in the study of Your Word, which results in a stronger faith that causes my heart to overflow with gratitude and daily thanksgiving. Amen.

_____
_____
_____
_____
_____
_____

JULY 2: THE FRUIT OF THE SPIRIT

> The Holy Spirit helps us develop spiritual fruit. When
> it is genuine, our character is not in dispute!

Galatians 5:22–23 (NIV) says, "But the fruit of the Spirit is love, joy, peace, patience, kindness, goodness, faithfulness, gentleness and self-control. Against such things there is no law."

These nine characteristics of spiritual fruit are produced in the believer as she or he yields to the obedience of the Holy Spirit of God. We cannot produce these on our own through human effort. But they are manifested in the life of the believer by the Spirit Himself.

Prayer

Lord, create in me a desire and determination to surrender my will and way to Your Spirit each day. I want my life to be pleasing to You. Let my fruit provide sweet nourishment in the lives of those I encounter each day. Thank You for cultivating my life into a fruit of righteousness that I and my family can enjoy. Amen.

JULY 3: CONTINUE IN THE FAITH YOU KNOW

Remain steadfast in what you believe, and a stronger
and more powerful faith you will receive!

In 2 Timothy 3:14–15 (NIV), we read, "But as for you, continue in what you have learned and have become convinced of, because you know those from whom you learned it, and how from infancy you have known the Holy Scriptures, which are able to make you wise for salvation through faith in Christ Jesus."

Remain faithful in the Word of God that you know. Do not allow anything or anyone to cause you to doubt what you believe about Jesus Christ. You have God's Word to continue to direct you and the Holy Spirit within to bear witness with your spirit of the love and faithfulness of the Lord. The study of the Word of God and prayer will allow you to continually grow in faith as you apply what you learn each day.

Prayer

Thank You, Lord, for Your faithfulness and continued guidance into a fuller understanding of Your Holy Word. Each day, allow Your Spirit to reveal to me deeper truths of who You are so that I may live better and share Your Word with others. Amen.

_____

_____

_____

_____

_____

_____

JULY 4: BE OF GOOD COURAGE

In the Lord—be strong, and He will give you a spiritual song!

Psalm 31:24 (NIV) says, "Be strong and take heart, all you who hope in the Lord."

Trials and testing will come in life, but when your faith is rooted in the hope of Jesus Christ, your heart will be strengthened in His love and confident that the Lord will be by your side. He is ever near today to give you comfort and blessed assurance when you need it.

Prayer

Lord, I love You and thank You too, for Your kind care and the sweet melodies of Your love that resonate in my spirit day by day. Amen.

JULY 5: I TRUST THAT YOU'RE MY GOD

Because the Lord is your God, you can trust Him,
for He will vindicate you and not condemn!

Psalm 31:14 (NIV) says, "But I trust in You, O Lord; I say, 'You are my God.'"

It is so sweet to trust in God, to rest in the assurance that all your needs, He will supply simply because you belong to Him and He genuinely cares for you.

Prayer

Lord, all my hopes and dreams rest in You. I have total confidence that every need, You will supply today because You are my God. In Jesus's name I pray. Amen.

JULY 6: SHINE ON ME AND SAVE ME

Shine down your favor upon me, and I'll
become all You desire me to be!

Psalm 31:16 (NIV) says, "Let Your face shine on Your servant; save
me in Your unfailing love."

The psalmist has total trust in the Lord, and now he asks for
God's divine favor to shine upon him to save him from his enemies
based on God's unfailing and endless love. God's love never fails;
He's always near to help us in times of need.

Prayer

Thank You for Your unfailing love toward me. Look upon me,
and let Your grace and mercy shine all around me, assuring me
that You are here with me today. I know that You won't leave me
to myself. Thank You for loving me, Jesus. Amen.

JULY 7: FAITHFUL GOD WON'T FORSAKE YOU

Faithful God won't forsake; He'll be there through every mistake!

Deuteronomy 4:31 (NIV) says, "For the Lord your God is a merciful God; He will not abandon or destroy you or forget the covenant with your forefathers, which He confirmed to them on oath."

Our God is tender and compassionate, like a mother caring for her infant child. When danger is near, she puts her arms around her child and holds it close. There is nothing that we can do that will cause the Lord to abandon us. As God made a covenant with Abraham, so He made a covenant with us through the blood of Jesus Christ to never leave us alone.

Prayer

Lord, thank You for Your compassion and loving care extended to me today and every day. I know You will not abandon me in times of need, but You will enfold me in Your arms of protection. You will draw closer to me to encourage and strengthen me where I'm weak. Thank You for loving me so much. Amen.

JULY 8: GOD IS NOT A MAN THAT HE SHOULD LIE

God cannot lie; if He did, He would have to die!

Numbers 23:19 (NIV) says, "God is not a man, that He should lie, nor a son of man, that He should change His mind. Does He speak and then not act? Does He promise and not fulfill?"

As imperfect humans, we are prone to lie to gain favor or advantage in unfavorable situations. Jesus was human and divine—Perfect Man and Perfect God. The Lord, being God, has no reason to change His mind because He knows all things and is able to do all things perfectly, and what He promises, he will bring to pass in His time. But we must maintain faith and trust in Him. Every need God will supply, and every promise, He will fulfill. Do you believe that God knows all things and controls all things?

Prayer

Thank You for being in control of my life. I surrender all that I am to You, O Lord. Let Your blessed will be done in my life today. I trust You to speak, act, and bring to pass the promises You have made to me. Amen.

_____

_____

_____

_____

_____

JULY 9: HOLD FAST TO YOUR PROFESSION OF FAITH

Hold fast to your profession of faith, for it will
determine just how well you run this race!

Hebrews 10:23 (NIV) says, "Let us hold unswervingly to the hope
we profess, for He who promised is faithful."

Hold fast to your faith in the Lord because it is tied to your
hope in Jesus Christ. Faith gives you the ability to grasp hope and
not let it go. Faith and hope will allow you to hold fast to the One
who is faithful and has promised never to leave or forsake His own.
Because we trust God, we have hope that His faithful promises
will manifest in our lives.

Prayer

Lord, I hold fast to the blessed hope that I have in Jesus Christ, who
is the Author and Finisher of my faith. Because I trust in You, I also
have hope that Your promises will be fulfilled in Your time. Amen.

_____
_____
_____
_____
_____
_____

JULY 10: HE IS FAITHFUL

Our God is faithful and true; continue to trust
Him, and He'll show you what to do!

In 2 Timothy 2:13 (NIV), we read, "If we are faithless, He will
remain faithful, for He cannot disown Himself."

Because we are human, we become afraid and grow weary on
this Christian journey. This scripture assures us that when we falter
in our faith, the Lord will still be faithful to us. He won't abandon
us or walk away, though we walk away from Him. He will go after
His own because we belong to Him, and the Lord cannot disown
us, for in so doing, He would disown Himself. His Holy Spirit
lives within our hearts. His love and faithfulness to His own mean
that He goes after us and brings us back to the fold. The Good
Shepherd cares for His own. Great is His faithfulness toward us.

Prayer

Thank You for Your faithfulness and love toward me. When I falter
and fail, You come after me and draw me close to Your precious
bleeding side. Lord, in Your love and mercy, hide me today. Reassure
me that I belong to You no matter what I do. Amen.

JULY 11: YOUR GOODNESS EXTENDED TO THOSE WHO TRUST

In order to experience God's goodness, trust in His Word is a must!

Psalm 31:19 (NIV) says, "How great is your goodness, which you have stored up for those who fear you, which you bestow in the sight of men."

How great and gracious is our God! His protection and faithfulness are beyond measure. When we think of His goodness toward us, praise should break forth in our hearts. Be confident that our God has greater things in store for those who belong to Him.

Prayer

Lord, I thank You for Your boundless love and provision bestowed upon me. Your goodness toward me is beyond comprehension. You are awesome, and I sense Your holy presence near me today. I have a future hope that rests in You, Jesus. Amen.

_____
_____
_____
_____
_____
_____

JULY 12: MY GOD, I PRAISE YOU

I praise You for who You are. You are near, when once You were far!

Isaiah 25:1 (NIV) says, "O Lord, You are my God; I will exalt You and praise Your name, for in perfect faithfulness You have done marvelous things, things planned long ago."

Isaiah praised God for the deliverance of His people. He declared that the Lord truly is his God based on the marvelous things He did to defend their cause. God promised His people long ago that He would protect them. All who know God will agree that He is faithful to His own. How has the Lord been faithful to you?

Prayer

Lord, thank You for Your faithfulness. I will open my mouth and will praise You all day long for delivering me from my trouble. Even when I am alone, I know that You are near, working out Your perfect plan for my good. Amen.

JULY 13: THOSE WHO KNOW YOU PRAISE YOU

I am Your child, and You know my name, and
Your gracious provisions, I claim!

Psalm 9:10 (NIV) says, "Those who know your name will trust in you, for you, Lord, have never forsaken those who seek you."

Because we know the Lord, we take refuge in His security and protection. We grow to trust in Him more and more as we study and meditate on His Holy Word. We pray and believe He will answer our prayers. The Lord promised to never leave us alone.

Prayer

Lord, I am so thankful that each day the Holy Spirit is revealing Your holy character to my spirit. I know Your name, and I'm so grateful for Your daily provisions. Thank You for keeping me today. Amen.

JULY 14: GOD HONORS WHAT HE SPEAKS

To every soul that seeks, the Holy Spirit speaks!

Psalm 89:34 (NIV) says, "I will not violate my covenant or alter what my lips have uttered."

God made a declaration to His covenant people (Israel) to assure them that He would keep His covenant promise. The Lord keeps His covenant promises to believers today as well. What God spoke in His Word will not return void. God promised Israel and the church also that He would continue to guide and protect them. He loves us all.

Prayer

Lord, You are merciful, loving, and kind. Your love is unconditional and sure; no matter what I do or say, You will not abandon me. Your Spirit speaks encouraging words to my heart. He reassures me that He is near and that He cares. Amen.

JULY 15: DON'T FEAR; HAVE FAITH

Don't be afraid, but make haste in trusting
God with an unwavering faith!

Mark 4:40 (NIV) says, "He said to his disciples, 'Why are you so afraid? Do you still have no faith?'"

Jesus assured His disciples that God's authority and power were present in Him. He was God in human flesh. He looked like men, but He was more than human. Jesus challenged them to believe—trust in Him. When faith is not present, fear abides. Perfect love casts out fear. Just believe!

Prayer

Lord, I trust and hope in You. Teach me to rest in You, my Savior and Lord. Help me overcome my doubts and fears and fill me with faith and trust in You. Amen.

_____
_____
_____
_____
_____
_____

JULY 16: HE DESIRES TO GIVE THE KINGDOM

God desires to provide your every need—
spiritual and physical; let Him lead!

Luke 12:32 (NIV) says, "Do not be afraid, little flock, for your Father has been pleased to give you the kingdom."

Jesus again tells His disciples not to fear, referring to them as "little flock" (a defenseless group that could be taken advantage of). Jesus tells them that because they seek Him, their needs will be provided. Therefore, they need not worry about anything because the kingdom is theirs. This truth applies to faithful believers today. Do you believe that He will provide for all your needs? Don't fear. Just believe!

Prayer

Lord, I desire Your spiritual blessings more than physical blessings. Uphold me with the right hand of Your power on every leaning side. Teach me Your ways so that I may obey Your decrees. I will not be afraid, but I will trust in You. Amen.

JULY 17: I WILL HOLD YOUR RIGHT HAND

To help you is God's plan—let Him hold your right hand!

Isaiah 41:13 (NIV) says, "For I am the Lord, your God, who takes hold of Your right hand and says to you, 'Do not fear; I will help you.'"

The Lord is our God; therefore, we do not have to fear. He will defend our cause and will take hold of our hand to guide and protect us from dangers seen and unseen because He is our Protector and Defender.

Prayer

Thank You, Lord, I am not fearful because I know that You are holding my hand and guiding me through all I must face today. Thank You for being my all in all. Amen.

_____
_____
_____
_____
_____

JULY 18: OBEY AND LIVE IN SAFETY

When you obey, you'll experience God's grace, and
the Spirit will move you to a safe place!

Proverbs 1:33 (NIV) says, "But whoever listens to me will live in safety, and be at ease, without fear of harm."

How wonderful it is to know that when you live a life that continues to please God, He will allow you to have peace without fear of harm. Yes, we'll be tried and tested on every side, but as we listen to the "still small voice" within, we know that God controls what comes into our lives. All things are filtered through His hands. Hallelujah!

Prayer

Lord, take my hand and lead me to a safe and quiet place, so that I may commune with You. Let me hear Your "still, small voice" as You speak life and strength to my heart. Amen.

JULY 19: A SPIRIT OF POWER, LOVE, AND SELF-CONTROL

Resist fear and allow the Lord to bless your soul
with power, love, and self-control!

In 2 Timothy 1:7 (NIV), we read, "For God did not give us a spirit of timidity, but a spirit of power, of love and of self-discipline."

We belong to the Lord. He calls us to respond to His Spirit. He has given us power, love, and self-control. A spirit of fear is not from the Lord. And because we belong to God, we can come boldly to His throne of grace and be assured that He will supply whatever we need. Utilize your faith to overcome your fears!

Prayer

Lord, allow a spirit of power, love, and self-control to rise up within my spirit. Fill me with Your Holy Spirit. Amen.

_____
_____
_____
_____
_____
_____

JULY 20: THE LORD IS MY HELPER

The Lord gives constant help, for by Him, we are kept!

Hebrews 13:6 (NIV) says, "So we say with confidence, 'The Lord is my Helper, I will not be afraid. What can man do to me?'"

When you trust in the Lord and commune with Him daily, you are able to say with holy, bold assurance that the Lord provides your every need. When trials come, you do not allow fear to cancel your faith, for you know that your God controls all things. Your Heavenly Father watches over you to help and defend.

Prayer

Lord, I depend on You to supply my needs. You are the only dependable help I know. In Your presence, I have no fear. Draw near to me as I draw near to You. In Jesus's name, I pray. Amen.

JULY 21: TRUST GOD AND BE SAFE

> When you trust God, you know that you are
> safe—He surrounds you with His grace!

Proverbs 29:25 (NIV) says, "Fear of man will prove to be a snare, but whoever trusts in the Lord is kept safe."

Where is your confidence? Do not put your trust in humankind; rather put your faith in the Living God. Only in Jesus Christ does one find a safe place. Learn to completely trust in the Lord.

Prayer

Lord, I put all my trust in You. I know You will never let me down. I have learned to lean and depend on You for all my needs. Thank You for keeping me safe. Amen.

JULY 22: GOD, OUR REFUGE AND STRENGTH

God is all you need. Rest in His arms as you let Him lead!

Psalm 46:1 (NIV) says, "God is our refuge and strength, an everpresent help in trouble."

The Lord is all you need. He will open doors and supply what you lack, but you must believe and keep your faith intact. Let Him guide and protect you. Let Him be your strong fortress of defense when trials come.

Prayer

Lord, You are all that I need today. I feel safe in Your loving arms. You provide the strength I need when I grow weak and weary. Continue to lead and guide me through various trials that I face. Amen.

JULY 23: DO NOT BE AFRAID; TOTALLY TRUST GOD

Don't be afraid, and don't be ashamed; lean on
Him totally, and His promises, claim!

Isaiah 54:4 (NIV) says, "Do not be afraid; you will not suffer shame. Do not fear disgrace; you will not be humiliated. You will forget the shame of your youth and remember no more the reproach of your widowhood."

This text was originally spoken to Israel to assure the nation that the Lord had not abandoned it. When you are mistreated and your faith is depleted, you can have the assurance that the Lord is with you. Whatever the situation you are facing, know that the Lord is there to calm your fears, dry your tears, and take away the shame or disgrace you may experience. His love for us has no limits or bounds. Jesus Christ died and rose from the dead to prove it.

Prayer

Lord, I will not fear anything of anyone but totally trust in You. You promised to be with me in all that I go through. You will take away my shame. Thank You for keeping me safe. Amen.

_____

_____

_____

_____

_____

JULY 24: YOU WILL PASS THROUGH

Whatever you face, you will pass through; God
will be there and come to your rescue!

Isaiah 43:2 (NIV) says, "When you pass through the waters, I will
be with you; and when you pass through the rivers, they will not
sweep over you. When you walk through the fire, you will not be
burned; the flames will not set you ablaze."

Because of the blood of Jesus, we are redeemed by God. Though
the floodwaters of life seek to overtake us, we will rise above them.
As we go through the fiery trials of life, we will not be set ablaze,
because the floodwaters will put out the fire as the Lord leads us
to safety. God is there, working behind the scenes for our good
and for His glory. We can trust and depend on the Lord to do all
He says He will do.

Prayer

Lord, there is no friend like You. Whatever befalls me, I know You
will be there to see me through it. Thank You for Your faithful love
and provisions. Amen.

JULY 25: BELIEVE WITHOUT SEEING

Faith demands that you believe without seeing.
Learn to trust God with your whole being!

John 20:29 (NIV) says, "Then Jesus told him, 'Because you have seen me, you have believed; blessed are those who have not seen and yet have believed.'"

Jesus spoke these words to one of His disciples (Thomas). Jesus challenged him to stop doubting and believe that He is God and that He rose from the dead. Like Thomas, we sometimes doubt the power of God. Jesus still calls us to a life of commitment and unwavering faith. He wants us to believe and trust in Him, so that our lives will be complete and full. Faith says believe it, and then you will see it!

Prayer

Lord, forgive my doubts and unbelief. Teach me to wholeheartedly trust in You and not in how things look or how I feel. I love You and thank You for keeping me. Amen.

JULY 26: ONCE YOUNG AND NOW OLD

Whether young or old, God loves and cares for every living soul!

Psalm 37:25 (NIV) says, "I was young and now I am old, yet I have never seen the righteous forsaken or their children begging bread."

God is gracious, and He provides for His own. He is a Father who supplies the needs of His children. No good thing will He withhold from those who love Him and who are called to fulfill His purpose. He is our Provider, who gives protection from harm. He makes a distinction between those who trust in Him and those who do not trust in Him.

Prayer

Lord, I love and trust You. All my needs You continue to provide. When I feel alone, You come alongside and guide me through each test. Thank You for Your kind care. Amen.

_____
_____
_____
_____
_____
_____

JULY 27: CAST YOUR BREAD UPON THE WATERS

Work your plan while you can to prepare for a future demand!

In Ecclesiastes 11:1 (NIV), we read, "Cast your bread upon the waters, for after many days you will find it again."

We live in a world of uncertainty; therefore, it is wiser to plan for the future than not to plan at all. When you prepare in your earlier days, many days (years) later, you will have something to hold on to in times of need. It is better to take action while you can than to live fearful of lack. Yes, we trust in the Lord, but we also plan for future needs. We are diligent in planning for physical needs. Do we exercise the same care when planning for your spiritual needs? The Lord will always do His part, and we must do what is assigned for us to do physically and spiritually. We are in partnership with the Lord.

Prayer

Lord, I thank You that my future is in Your hands. But give me wisdom to prepare now for what I may need later. You know my path and order my steps. By faith, I will do my part and leave the rest to You. Amen.

_____

_____

_____

_____

_____

_____

JULY 28: GOD BLESSES YOUR CHILDREN BECAUSE OF YOU

God will bless you because you are faithful and
true and also those who hang around you!

Isaiah 44:3 (NIV) says, "For I will pour water on the thirsty land, and streams on the dry ground; I will pour out my Spirit on your offspring and my blessing on your descendants."

This text speaks of physical and spiritual revival for Israel. God has not changed; we too can have a physical and spiritual awakening by turning back to God in obedience and by renewing our faith and trust in Him. God promises to pour out blessings like streams of water on a dry and thirsty terrain. As we meditate on His Word and resolve to apply its principles to daily living, we will be revived spiritually and renewed physically. Our children too will benefit from the blessings of the Lord on our behalf.

Prayer

Lord, revive me again with Your Holy Spirit. Draw me nearer to Your precious bleeding side as I surrender myself anew to You. Provide for the physical needs. Bless my family today. Fill me now. In Jesus's name, I pray. Amen.

_____
_____
_____
_____
_____
_____

JULY 29: THE LORD SAVES

The Lord is the One who saves; He makes your enemies behave!

Psalm 138:7 says, "Though I walk in the midst of trouble, you preserve my life; you stretch out your hand against the anger of my foes, with your right hand you save me."

Whatever situation you are in, God is able to bring you through it. He leads, guides, and protects all who trust in Him as they walk in His way. He will defend your cause against your enemies. Trust in the Lord, and wait on Him.

Prayer

In times of trouble, hide me in Your protective arms. When my enemies come up against me, I will not fear, but my confidence rests in You. Lift me up today and give me Your peace that passes human understanding. Thank You for loving me. Amen.

JULY 30: GOD IS GOOD, AND HE CARES

> God is good, and He cares; to those who trust
> Him, blessing after blessing, He shares!

Nahum 1:7 (NIV) says, "The Lord is good, a refuge in times of trouble. He cares for those who trust in Him."

God brings judgment on those who oppose Him, but He is good to those who trust in Him. He provides refuge from the storms of life, as He protects us from danger. God is good to those who love Him and are called by His name.

Prayer

You are a good God. When trials and trouble come, You hide me under the protective shadow of your wings. Thank You, Lord for caring for me and my family. Amen.

JULY 31: SALVATION OF THE RIGHTEOUS

Salvation and righteousness are of God. Give Him your whole heart!

Psalm 37:39 (NIV) says, "The salvation of the righteous comes from the Lord; He is their stronghold in times of trouble."

Our salvation was purchased by Jesus Christ on the cross of Calvary, and it was revealed by the empty tomb on resurrection morning. He rose with all power in His hands, and all we need for salvation is already supplied. Jesus Christ paid it all. He is our fortress, rock, and stronghold in times of need. Trust and believe, and you will receive God's protection, provision, and power to rise above any problem that confronts you.

Prayer

Lord, You are my Savior and a fence of protection around me. You are also my stronghold, as You protect me from the evil that surrounds me. Thank You for every need supplied. Amen.

_____
_____
_____
_____
_____
_____

AUGUST

And pray for one another, so that you will be healed.
—James 5:16 (NIV)

A PRAYER FOR YOU

Today I said a prayer for you!
I called out your name.
His promises are sure, and
Each one you can claim.
For the God we serve is forever
And always the same.

I said a prayer for you that the Lord,
The God of all comfort, will touch
And heal your body.
Whatever the outcome, let your
Praise and thanksgiving be hardy.
For God alone is worthy of all praise
And glory.

Today I said a prayer for you that God
Would comfort you and each trial
He will continually see you through.

I said a prayer for you that you will feel
His love and care. And be assured that
Jesus is always there.

Shirley A. Howard

AUGUST 1: WHY ARE YOU DOWNCAST, O MY SOUL?

No need to be downcast, O my soul—you belong to God's fold!

Psalm 42:11 (NIV) says, "Why are you downcast, O my soul? Why so disturbed within me? Put your hope in God, for I will yet praise Him, my Savior and my God."

When you belong to the Lord and you are walking in the truth of His Word, there is no need to be downcast because God has things under His control. Reflect on the trust and hope that you have in the Lord. Then begin to praise your way through the storm that you are experiencing until the Son-light shines through. Meditate on the goodness of the Lord, and allow the Holy Spirit to lift you up!

Prayer

Lord, I praise Your holy and righteous name. I lift Your name on high. Fill my heart with the joy that only comes from You. This I ask in Jesus's name. Amen.

_____
_____
_____
_____
_____
_____

AUGUST 2: THROUGH CHRIST, YOU BELIEVE IN GOD

Through Jesus, we get a glimpse of Father God—
open up and receive Him into your heart!

In 1 Peter 1:21 (NIV), we read, "Through Him you believe in God, who raised Him from the dead and glorified Him and so your faith and hope are in God."

We come to know and trust in God because of His Son, Jesus Christ. He, being God, became human and grew into a man who did only what His Father told Him to do. He died on a cross and was buried. The Father resurrected Him from the dead and glorified Him by His ascension into heaven. Christ is coming back one day to rule and reign for a thousand years, and then eternity will begin. Because of Christ, we have everlasting life and will live with Him in eternity.

Prayer

Father God, I thank You for Your Son. Lord Jesus, thank You for dying for my sins and giving me eternal life here and now. Today, I rejoice because I have a blessed hope and a glorious future forevermore with You. Amen.

AUGUST 3: A LIVING HOPE REQUIRES A LIVING FAITH

A living hope brings forth a present joy
that this old world can't destroy!

In 1 Peter 1:6 (NIV), we read, "In this you greatly rejoice, though now for a little while you may have had to suffer grief in all kinds of trials."

When there is a living hope (faith), the present joy within brings comfort and assurance in Jesus Christ. This kind of faith can enable believers to rejoice even when they are called on to suffer grief in all kinds of trials. The trials themselves are seen as occasions for joy. Tribulations draw us closer to the Lord. We don't always understand, but we learn to trust and wait on God.

Prayer

Lord Jesus, You are my Blessed Hope. Because of Your Holy Word, I have faith in You. I surrender my life and will to You. Amen.

_____

_____

_____

_____

_____

AUGUST 4: PURE MAKES SURE

Because Christ is pure, and we are His, our salvation is sure!

In 1 John 3:3 (NIV), we read, "Everyone who has this hope in him purifies himself, just as He is pure!"

The hope that we have is that one day we will be like Christ because we became children of God when we first believed and received the Holy Spirit within our hearts. Because we are saved by hope in Christ, inwardly, we are purified (complete) just as Christ is. His righteousness is given to us by the indwelling Holy Spirit.

Prayer

Thank You for Your indwelling Holy Spirit, who keeps me holy, pure, and at peace because of Jesus Christ, my Savior and the Lord of my life. Amen.

AUGUST 5: CHRIST, THE HOPE OF GLORY

Christ within me empowers me to tell the Gospel story!

Colossians 1:27 (NIV) says, "To them God has chosen to make known among the gentiles the glorious riches of this mystery, which is Christ in you, the hope of glory."

Because of Christ's death and resurrection, all believers stand at the same level before Him. At first, it was to Jews only; now all believers have this right and have received the indwelling Holy Spirit. This is the mystery hidden in the Old Testament—the church is the body of Christ. Jesus Christ is in us, the hope of glory.

Prayer

Thank You, Lord, for saving me. Thank You for Your indwelling Holy Spirit, who teaches and guides me into a fuller understanding of Your truth. Amen.

_____
_____
_____
_____
_____
_____

AUGUST 6: HOPE IN THE LORD

Hope in the Lord leads to a clear scope of who He is!

Lamentations 3:25 (NIV) says, "The Lord is good to those whose hope is in Him, to the one who seeks Him."

A steadfast faith will lead to a steadfast hope in God. When afflictions come, we endure them with hope in God's salvation. He will restore us in His time, because God's compassion and love will lift us and His mercies are new every day.

Prayer

Lord, my hope is in You. My faith will not falter because, in all things, I trust You to keep me in perfect peace when my mind is focused on You. Amen.

AUGUST 7: THE GOD OF HOPE FILLS US WITH JOY

> Faith and trust in God gives hope and joy
> that this world can never destroy!

Romans 15:13 (NIV) says, "May the God of hope fill you with all joy and peace as you trust in Him, so that you may overflow with hope by the power of the Holy Spirit."

Our God is the God of Hope. The biblical word teaches us that "everything written in the past was written to teach us, so that through endurance and encouragement of the Scriptures, we will have hope" (verse 4).

Prayer

Jesus, You are my Blessed Hope. In You, there is no lack. My trust is in the love You showed at Calvary when you died and rose from the grave to guarantee my hope. Thank You for loving me so. Amen.

AUGUST 8: RESTORE DOUBLE HOPE

Trust in the Lord, hope in Him, and receive double for your trouble!

Zechariah 9:12 (NIV) says, "Return to your fortress, O prisoners of hope; even now I announce that I will restore twice as much to you."

The prophet tells wayward Israel (this applies to the church today) to come back to the place of safety. Their hope is in God's faithful promise to them. We too have hope in Christ's faithfulness to us. In our afflictions, we are drawn closer to God, which is also a blessing. He will give double blessings for each trouble or affliction.

Prayer

Lord, my trust and hope is in You forever. All my days, I will give You praise and thanksgiving. Please bless all people who delight in Your name. And those who do not believe, may they come to a saving knowledge of who You are. Amen.

AUGUST 9: YOU HEAR OUR CRY

Because You hear our faintest cry; on You,
our Blessed Hope, we totally rely!

Psalm 10:17 (NIV) says, "You hear, O Lord, the desire of the afflicted; you encourage them, and you listen to their cry."

Because the Lord hears the prayers of His children who are suffering, you can be confident that He will move on your behalf. We trust in Him and in hope wait for Him to deliver us.

Prayer

Thank You, Lord, for being my hope when things seem hopeless. Hear my cry, dear Lord, and rescue me from all my afflictions. Amen.

AUGUST 10: HUMBLE AS A CHILD

Greatness is not a matter of what you say or do,
but a matter of a lowly spirit of humility!

Matthew 18:4 (NIV) says, "Therefore, whoever humbles himself like this child is the greatest in the kingdom of heaven."

Greatness in God's kingdom is not based on the standard of the world system. Greatness in the kingdom of heaven is not based on good deeds or political or economic standing; the kingdom of heaven is based on humility or childlike faith in God. It consists of love, peace, and joy in the Holy Spirit.

Prayer

Lord, give me a spirit of humility so that I may please You in all that I do. Thank You for loving and keeping me. Give me a mind and heart to share Your love with all I meet. Amen.

AUGUST 11: GRACE TO THE HUMBLE

Humble yourself before Holy God and
receive more grace to run life's race!

James 4:6 (NIV) says, "But he gives us more grace. This is why Scripture says: 'God opposes the proud but gives grace to the humble.'"

God opposes (battles against) those who are proud—thinking more highly of themselves than they ought. But to the humble, our God gives grace (undeserved favor). We can resist pride by seeking the Lord first, before our own desires. Humility is rooted in faith and trust in God. Who is the object of your faith?

Prayer

Lord, I humbly submit my will to You today. Have Your way in my life. I submit my life under Your authority. Thank You for all You do for me and my family. Amen.

_____
_____
_____
_____
_____
_____

AUGUST 12: HUMILITY AND REVERENCE

> Humility is the way; reverence of God will be
> maintained as long as you study, pray, and obey!

Proverbs 22:4 (NIV) says, "Humility and the fear of the Lord bring wealth and honor and life."

When we humbly trust, obey, and rely on the Lord, He will provide our needs. Humility comes into a heart that is committed to the worship and adoration of the Lord. As we learn to reverence God, humility becomes a by-product of faith. When our love and respect for God come first, it opens the door to wealth, honor, and a joyful life that is centered on Christ. Even though we are not exempt from trials and trouble, we are assured that we never walk the journey alone. God is there as we humbly yield to His sovereign will.

Prayer

Lord, I humbly trust and obey You. You hold first place in my heart and in my daily walk and talk. Continue to draw me closer to Christ's precious bleeding side. Amen.

AUGUST 13: REVERENCE AND HONOR

A wise person honors God, and a humble person is near His heart!

Proverbs 15:33 (NIV) says, "The fear of the Lord teaches a man wisdom, and humility comes before honor."

To fear God means to reverence (trust, obey, serve, worship) Him. All who fear God learn wisdom. Godly wisdom (the truth coupled with just judgment—knowing what is right and doing it) flows from our reverence for God. Humility opens the door to honor. As previously stated, humility is a by-product of faith. Scripture tells us that without faith, we can't please God. All who live a life that pleases God will be honored by Him. How are you living your life?

Prayer

Lord, I choose to worship and serve You with a humble heart. Give me wisdom to trust and obey You as I humbly serve those less fortunate than I. Give me discernment that I may know Your heart and live my life in total reverence to You. Amen.

_____

_____

_____

_____

_____

_____

AUGUST 14: JOY IS IN THE LORD

> The Lord is my joy and my strength; only
> in Him am I totally content!

Nehemiah 8:10c (NIV) says, "Do not grieve, for the joy of the Lord is your strength."

When trouble comes, we have a choice—worry or trust the Lord. When we lay our petitions out before God, He will take care of the problem. Worry and fretting does not change the matter. We can trust God, by recognizing that complete trust brings joy. The joy that we have in Him becomes our enduring strength and motivation to go on.

Prayer

Lord, thank You for the blessed assurance in my heart that You will meet all my needs. I take joy in knowing that when I pray, You hear and will answer. Thank you for the joy that I feel today. Amen.

AUGUST 15: JOY AND PEACE

Joy and peace come when, in Jesus Christ, you have total belief!

Isaiah 55:12 (NIV) says, "You will go out in joy and be led forth in peace; the mountains and hills will burst into song before you, and all the trees of the field will clap their hands."

Isaiah speaks of a future time during the Millennium when the effects of sin will be reversed (fall of Adam and Eve, Genesis 3:17–19). When Jesus returns, all of creation will rejoice as the curse of the physical creation is broken and its original beauty is restored. This will be a joyful time. However, as the redeemed of God, we can know peace and joy now and sing songs of praise for what Christ has already done by dying on the cross and rising from the dead. Rejoice in the Lord, and be glad!

Prayer

Thank You, Jesus, for the peace and joy in my heart because of Your love for us. I praise You today and will praise Your name forever. Amen.

AUGUST 16: GREATER JOY IS IN THE LORD

Greater joy comes when total trust in God, we learn to deploy!

Psalm 4:7 (NIV) says, "You have filled my heart with greater joy than when their grain and new wine abound."

David expressed that the joy and contentment that he had in God was greater than any material benefit he would receive. The Lord held first place in David's heart. Where is your greatest joy found?

Prayer

Lord, I desire You more than my necessary food. Only You can fill the deep hunger of my soul. Thank You for Your provisions. Amen.

_____
_____
_____
_____
_____
_____

AUGUST 17: SOW IN TEARS, REAP IN JOY

Tears will turn to joy as you trust in God; learn to
love and obey Him with your whole heart!

Psalm 126:6 (NIV) says, "He who goes out weeping, carrying seed
to sow, will return with songs of joy, carrying sheaves with him."

To sow in tears refers to agonizing over the work at hand to
further the kingdom of God. For the church, it could include basic
activities, such as sharing your faith with others, serving those who
have needs, participating in helping those less fortunate, giving
of your finances, or spending time encouraging children or the
elderly. God's work can be time-consuming, but when we persist
in planting the seed (God's Word shared with others or prayer for
others), a harvest will come eventually. Some seed will fall on good
ground, and some will fall on rocky soil. God gives the increase.
The harvest will yield much rejoicing when people hear the Word
and are saved. Quitting is not an option. Pray to the Lord of the
harvest for a bountiful crop.

Prayer

Lord, help me recognize and take advantage of every opportunity
to share the Good News of salvation with others. Give them
attentive ears to hear and receive the gospel message. Teach me how
to intercede in prayer for others. In Jesus's name, I pray. Amen.

AUGUST 18: COMPLETE JOY IN JESUS

> Only the joy in Jesus makes us complete, because
> it gives us access to His mercy seat!

John 15:11 (NIV) says, "I have told you this so that my joy may be in you, and that your joy may be complete."

Jesus told His disciples, "If you obey My commands, you will remain in My love, just as I have obeyed My Father and remain in His Love" (verse 10). Our joy rests in our ability to remain in Christ's love. We remain in Him by obeying Him. By remaining in Him, we will also learn to extend love and kindness to others.

Prayer

Help me to remain in Your love by obeying Your commands and showing lovingkindness to others. Thank You for loving me. Amen.

AUGUST 19: JOYFUL IN THE LORD

> My joy is in the Lord, my Savior and King;
> each day, He gives me a song to sing!

Habakkuk 3:18 (NIV) says, "Yet I will rejoice in the Lord. I will be joyful in God my Savior."

In whatever state we are in, we can be joyful in the Lord—not necessarily with the situation itself but in the fact that God cares and will never leave us alone. He is able to sustain us in every situation when we trust in Him. He is our inexhaustible source of infinite joy.

Prayer

In all things, Lord, give me joy that flows from Your heart to mine. Give me endurance power to wait on You. Amen.

AUGUST 20: WE TRUST; WE REJOICE

Because we trust in God, we have joy in our heart!

Psalm 33:21(NIV) says, "In Him our hearts rejoice, for we trust in His holy name."

Because our faith and trust are in the Lord, we wait in hope, we rejoice in Him, and we rest in His unfailing love, which is always available to us.

Prayer

Lord, You are my confident hope that all I entrust to you will be fulfilled by faith in Jesus's name. Amen.

_____

_____

_____

_____

_____

AUGUST 21: REJOICE FOR SALVATION AND RIGHTEOUSNESS

We delight in His salvation and righteousness
by living for Him in faithfulness!

Isaiah 61:10a (NIV) says, "I delight greatly in the Lord; my soul rejoices in my God. For He has clothed me with garments of salvation and arrayed me in a robe of righteousness."

Salvation and righteousness are the clothes that the child of God wears. We have been saved by Jesus Christ; therefore, we take great delight in Him, and our soul rejoices.

Prayer

How I love you, O Lord, my Savior and the Perfector of my faith and righteousness. I rejoice and delight in Your holy name. Amen.

AUGUST 22: THE UPRIGHT IN HEART GIVE PRAISE

The upright give praises because God's grace totally amazes!

Psalm 64:10 (NIV) says, "Let the righteous rejoice in the Lord and take refuge in Him; let all the upright in heart praise Him."

The righteous rejoice in the Lord and take refuge in the Lord because they trust in Him. They obey God's commands; they praise and worship Him for His provision, protection, and power to keep them safe.

Prayer

Lord, I rejoice in Your name; You are my God and my shelter from the storms of life. Thank You for being with me in all that I go through. Amen.

AUGUST 23: THE MIGHTY GOD IS WITH YOU

God is with you to save; open your heart and give Him joyful praise!

Zephaniah 3:17a (NIV) says, "The Lord your God is with you, He is mighty to save."

When you trust in the Lord with all your heart and obey His words, He is mighty to save from hurt, harm, and dangers. As we study the Bible and pray, we learn to trust His judgments and walk in His ways.

Prayer

Lord, You are my Mighty God, and there is nobody like You. I put all my trust in You. Uphold me with the right hand of Your righteousness and power. Amen!

AUGUST 24: LIVE IN LOVE, LIVE IN GOD

God is love, and when you live in God, you'll have His heart!

In 1 John 4:16 (NIV), we read, "And so we know and rely on the love God has for us. God is love. Whoever lives in love lives in God; and God in him."

As believers, we have a personal knowledge of God's love through continual experiences of faith, which prove that God loves us unconditionally. Because God is love and we abide in His love, He lives in us.

Prayer

Lord, thank You for my confident trust in You. I am learning to obey and abide in You, as You abide in me. Lord, I rejoice in Your love for me today. Amen.

_____

_____

_____

_____

_____

_____

AUGUST 25: HE LOVED US FIRST

God loved us first; He sent His Son to save the inhabitants of earth!

In 1 John 4:19 (NIV), we read, "We love because He first loved us."

We know that we love God when we trust and obey Him. The love that we have first originated with God, and it flows from Him to us. And because His love resides in our heart, we are able to extend the love of Jesus to others.

Prayer

Father, thank You for loving me so much. You are giving me hope and a future. I love You today and always. Continue to provide me with opportunities to show forth Your love to others. Amen.

AUGUST 26: ENJOY GREAT PEACE

The humble and meek will enjoy peace because
it's Holy God whom they seek!

Psalm 37:11 (NIV) says, "But the meek will inherit the land and enjoy great peace."

God exalts the humble of heart. Blessings will come when we humble ourselves under the mighty hand of God by obeying His commands. We learn to show love and compassion to others.

Prayer

Lord, as I humbly obey Your Word and walk in Your way, I find peace each day that I trust in You. Thank You, Lord. Amen.

AUGUST 27: ENDLESS PRAISE

Endless praise to our God that's forever
and always from a joyful heart!

Psalm 22:26 (NIV) says, "The poor will eat and be satisfied; they who seek the Lord will praise Him—may your hearts live forever."

Our God is worthy of praise for who He is. God is concerned for all people, rich and poor and those afflicted in any way. Because God is God, our praise to Him should never end. God's love extends to the physically poor and the poor in spirit. What is your need?

Prayer

Lord, I praise You because You are my God and worthy of continual praise. Today, I offer to You heartfelt praise and thanksgiving. Amen.

AUGUST 28: WE DELIGHT IN THE LORD

The Lord is our delight. We take courage in Him,
because, for our cause, He will fight!

Psalm 149:4 (NIV) says, "For the Lord takes delight in His people;
He crowns the humble with salvation."

We praise the Lord for who He is, but also because He takes pleasure in us and gives us salvation. He is able to save us from all harm. Eternal and abundant life rest in Jesus Christ alone.

Prayer

Thank You, Lord, for Your lovingkindness and tender care. Each day, You are near to guide and encourage me along the way. Thank You for the abundant life, peace, and joy that I have today. Amen!

AUGUST 29: GOD OF COMPASSION

> We have a God of compassion who desires to bless;
> He faithfully leads us through each test!

Isaiah 30:18 (NIV) says, "Yet the Lord longs to be gracious to you; He rises to show you compassion. For the Lord is a God of justice. Blessed are all who wait for Him."

The Lord loves us and desires to be gracious and compassionate. He is the God of justice, and He blesses those who trust and rely on Him. He also expects us to show kindness and compassion toward others. By faith, learn to wait patiently for the Lord, for He rewards those who are faithful and true.

Prayer

Thank You for loving me and showing compassion for me. I'm grateful for each daily blessing you give. Help me to be kinder and more compassionate to others so that Your love can be seen in and through me. Amen.

_____

_____

_____

_____

_____

_____

AUGUST 30: COMPASSIONATE FATHER

God is compassionate toward us because in
our weakness, we are but dust!

Psalm 103:13 (NIV) says, "As a father has compassion on his children, so the Lord has compassion on those who fear (reverence) Him."

God knows us well; our Father knows all of our weaknesses. He is always near, is concerned, and cares for us. He knows that we lean and depend on Him, and He will not leave us all alone. He is always there.

Prayer

Lord, continue to show compassion on me. You know the frailty of my human body and mind. Strengthen me and give me Your heart. Give me renewed strength in my weakest hour. Amen.

AUGUST 31: EVERLASTING LOVE

You love us with an everlasting love that pours down from above!

Psalm 103:17a (NIV) says, "But from everlasting to everlasting the Lord's love is with those who fear (reverence) Him."

There are no limits and no end to the love that the Lord has for those who belong to Him. Those who trust and obey will always have favor with Him. His grace endures forever!

Prayer

Thank You for meeting each one of my needs today. Your love for me is unending, and Your mercy abides forever. I love You, Lord. Amen.

_____
_____
_____
_____
_____
_____

SEPTEMBER

Praise the Lord. Praise God in his sanctuary; praise
him in his mighty heavens. Praise him for his acts of
power; praise him for his surpassing greatness … Let
everything that has breath praise the Lord.
—Psalm 150: 1, 2, 6 (NIV)

YOUR NAME ON HIGH

Lord, I lift Your name up high;
I shout it above the earth and sky!

Praise, worship, and thanksgiving
Is due Your name,
For in You all promises we claim!

In Your holy presence, peace and
Joy we find; even in times of stress
And confusion, we see the truth of
This paradigm!

I lift Your name above the heavens,
And the sound of it resonates above
The earth, giving lost people second
Birth!

Shirley A. Howard

SEPTEMBER 1: PRAISE AND THANKSGIVING TO MY GOD

The Lord is my God; I love Him with all of my heart!

Psalm 118:28 (NIV) says, "You are my God, and I will give you thanks; you are my God, and I will exalt you."

Because of what Jesus did at Calvary and the empty tomb, we give Him all praise and thanksgiving for saving our souls. We exalt His name every chance we get because of His faithful and compassionate love toward us, even while we were still sinners. Reflect upon what the Lord has done for you, and give Him praise.

Prayer

Lord, You are my mighty God. You are always there when I need you. Today, I give praise and thanksgiving to You. You are worthy of all praise. Thank you for loving me and my family. Amen.

SEPTEMBER 2: WHEN GOD IS SILENT

> Though God is silent, yet He speaks; the salvation
> of humankind is what He seeks!

Job 34:29 (NIV) says, "But if he remains silent, who can condemn him? If he hides his face, who can see him? Yet he is over man and nation alike."

We may wonder why God allows injustice to exist. We pray and seemingly God does not hear. Because of the suffering and pain in the world, we may ask why God looks away. Does He not see? Does He not care? Our Sovereign cares about all of His creation. He is holy and righteous, loving and compassionate. He sees the wickedness, and for a while, He chooses to do nothing. He desires all to repent and be saved. In His sovereignty, God rules over humankind and nations. And in His own time, He will judge all sin and unrighteousness.

Prayer

Sovereign Lord, please hear my cry for justice in this world. There is so much pain and suffering that surround me. Deliver those who are in turmoil and pain. Speak peace and protection into their situation. Hide Your face from them no longer. Let Your grace and mercy prevail in their lives. Let Your love shine forth as the sun, bringing warmth to the soul. This I ask in the name of Jesus. Amen.

SEPTEMBER 3: PEACE AT ALL TIMES AND IN EVERY WAY

At all times and every way, I have Your peace
because in Your Word, rests my belief!

In 2 Thessalonians 3:16 (NIV), we read, "Now may the Lord of peace himself give you peace at all times and in every way. The Lord be with all of you."

Jesus Christ is our peace. When we put our trust in Him and obey His commands, we will experience His peace in our lives. He is the Prince of Peace. He offers us peace that defies human understanding. He gives a peace and calm assurance that this world cannot give. Peace originated in the person of Jesus Christ. Praise God!

Prayer

Lord, thank You for Your Holy Word. As I study and obey it, Your peace calms my soul and spirit. Thank You for giving me peace today. You are my Prince of Peace, and I praise Your holy and righteous name. Amen.

EVERY DAY WITH JESUS

SEPTEMBER 4: YOUR FAITH SAVES YOU

It is your faith that saves, without it; you're
doomed to an eternal grave!

Luke 7:50 (NIV) says, "Jesus said to the woman, 'Your faith has
saved you: go in peace.'"

Jesus is no respecter of persons. All who believe His Word and
invite Jesus into their heart will be saved and will have eternal life.
Faith is the act of believing and obeying the Lord.

Prayer

Father, thank You for Jesus Christ, who died and rose from the
dead so that I may have eternal life. Strengthen me so that I will
continue to worship You and obey Your Word each day. Empower
me that I may win souls for Your kingdom. Amen.

SEPTEMBER 5: DON'T FEAR—TRUST

God desires your good; unexpected things in life—
don't fear. He will wipe away each tear!

Luke 12:32 (NIV) says, "Do not be afraid, little flock, for your
Father has been pleased to give you the kingdom."

Jesus tells us not to be afraid of challenges that confront us.
He knows what we can bear, and He desires to give us what is best.
Turn your fear into trust; believe that Christ will be with you in
all that you face. When you have Jesus on your side, you have the
kingdom of heaven as backup! Thank You, Jesus!

Prayer

Lord, I trust You to provide all that I need and to protect me from
harm. I trust You to do what is best. Give me courage to stand firm
against each test. Amen

SEPTEMBER 6: GOD WILL HEAR AND ANSWER YOUR CRY

Your cry for help is heard by God as it travels beyond the sky!

Isaiah 30:19 (NIV) says, "O people of Zion, who live in Jerusalem, you will weep no more. How gracious he will be when you cry for help! As soon as he hears, he will answer you."

God promised Israel that their time of weeping would end and He would answer their prayers speedily. He says the same to His church in this century. God desires for His people to dwell in safety and peace. As we turn to Him in faithful obedience, He will hear and answer our prayers in a timely manner. Don't allow your faith and trust in the Lord to falter; rather draw closer to Him in meditation and fervent prayer. Believe the Lord, and do not doubt (Mark 11:24).

Prayer

Lord, order my steps today in my going and coming. Sanctify my heart and mind that I may be pleasing to You. Thank You for Your protection, peace, and love. Thank You for wiping away the tears from my eyes. I know that You hear and You will answer. Amen.

SEPTEMBER 7: GOD ENABLES ME TO STAND

The Lord gives me strength to stand. Each
step is guided by His hand!

Habakkuk 3:19 (NIV) says, "The Sovereign Lord is my strength;
He makes my feet like the feet of a deer, He enables me to go on
the heights."

God is all-knowing, and He strengthens those who trust in Him
by giving them the ability to overcome trials and tests. Trust Him
today. Ask the Lord, and He will strengthen your faith so you will
be able to handle all the trials that you face. In Christ Jesus, there
is nothing you cannot do. He has given you power and strength;
step out by faith and achieve what God has planned for you.

Prayer

Thank You for daily strength and the necessary provisions each
day. By faith, I receive all that You have assigned my hands to do
in Your holy name. Amen.

_____
_____
_____
_____
_____
_____

SEPTEMBER 8: THE WORD AND HEALING

> Without the Word of God, there is no faith. But the
> Word of God and healing faith, you can trace!

Luke 9:11 (NIV) says, "He welcomed them and spoke to them about the Kingdom of God, and healed those who needed healing."

Jesus provided the needs of the crowd of people around Him. Salvation comes by faith in God. Faith moves one to be healed when one sells out to God! Perseverance is a necessary quality in the life of a believer. And a steadfast trust in the Word is a must, if one desires to be healed. Do you wholly trust in Jesus Christ?

Prayer

Thank You, Lord, for Your faithfulness and love. Please provide my basic needs today. I believe that all power rests in Your hands. Heal my body and make me whole, in the name of Jesus. Amen.

SEPTEMBER 9: YOU CALL, AND HE ANSWERS

The Lord will answer when you call; just
believe and let your faith stand tall!

Psalm 138:3 (NIV) says, "When I called, you answered me; you
made me bold and stouthearted."

David promised to praise the Lord with his whole heart because
the Lord answered his prayer and caused his faith to be strengthened.
Reflect upon how the Lord has delivered you in times of need.

Prayer

Thank You, Lord, for granting me the boldness and strength to
stand with assurance that because You heard my prayers, the answer
is on the way. So, I thank You in advance. Amen.

_____

_____

_____

_____

_____

SEPTEMBER 10: BE STRONG AND COURAGEOUS

No need to fear, by faith you know God is
near! (He lives within your heart.)

Deuteronomy 31:6 (NIV) says, "Be strong and courageous. Do
not be afraid or terrified because of them, for the Lord your God
goes with you; He will never leave you nor forsake you."

God's Word encourages us to be strong and not be afraid.
Whether we turn to the left or right, forward or back, the Lord is
there and won't leave us alone. Trust Him, and allow His presence
to uphold and strengthen you.

Prayer

Lord, thank You for Your constant presence and protection in
all that I go through in this life. I know You are here with me;
therefore, I will not worry or fear. Amen.

SEPTEMBER 11: GOD IS ALL AROUND

> Lord, I have confident faith that You are all around, and
> the strongholds of the devil, You will bring down!

Psalm 34:7 (NIV) says, "The Angel of the Lord encamps around
those who fear Him, and He delivers them."

David declares that the Lord Himself encamps around us
or provides protection for all who reverence Him. The Lord will
protect His own. You must believe and not doubt that the Lord is
the shield of protection all around you, so the enemy will not be
able to cause you to fear.

Prayer

Lord, thank You for watching over me today. I am confident that
You dispatched Your angel to protect me from the snares of the
enemy. I rely on You to protect me from harm. Amen.

SEPTEMBER 12: THE LORD IS ...

The Lord is all you need Him to be—Christ died to set us free!

Psalm 27:1 (NIV) says, "The Lord is my light and my salvation—whom shall I fear? The Lord is the stronghold of my life—of whom shall I be afraid?"

Like David, we can express a confident faith that the Lord will deliver us from harm, because He is our light, salvation, and a stronghold in times of trouble.

Prayer

Thank You, Lord, for being everything that I need when I need it. I will not be fearful of anything, but I will trust in Your provisions. Thank You for saving me. Amen.

SEPTEMBER 13: THE LORD REFRESHES AND SATISFIES

The Lord will refresh and satisfy—lift up
holy hands to God and glorify!

Jeremiah 31:25 (NIV) says, "I will refresh the weary and satisfy
the faint."

Are you weary and faint of heart? Put all your trust in the Lord,
and He will refresh you. Your body, soul, and spirit will be satisfied
by the Lord. He loves you unconditionally.

Prayer

Lord, when I am weary, You give refreshment. When I feel weak,
You satisfy me with Your goodness. Thank You for sustaining and
keeping me today. Amen.

SEPTEMBER 14: CREATION REVEALS GOD

God created all, so humankind would revere
Him, and on His name call!

Acts 17:27 (NIV) says, "God did this so that men would seek Him and perhaps reach out for Him and find Him, though He is not far from each one of us."

God is the Maker and Creator of this world. He created every person so that we will know who He is and will worship Him. When we were saved, the Holy Spirit took up residence within. Therefore, God is always near us, He lives in our heart. Allow Him to empower and strengthen you today. Look around you and see God's handy work.

Prayer

Holy Father and Creator, I thank You for loving me before I knew You. And You sought after me and drew me safely and tenderly into Your arms. Now, I am forever in Your presence. Thank You, Holy Spirit! Amen.

_____
_____
_____
_____
_____
_____

SEPTEMBER 15: LORD, YOU ARE MINE

The Creator of all things is mine. No greater love or honor can I find!

Lamentations 3:24 (NIV) says, "I say to myself, 'The Lord is my portion; therefore, I will wait for Him.'"

Great is God's lovingkindness to us. His mercies are new every day and are in endless supply. So, despite the circumstance we may face, God's supply is endless. Therefore, I will wait on Him and be satisfied!

Prayer

Thank You for Your faithful love toward me. You are my portion. I can eat of the living bread from heaven until I want no more. Your love and care is boundless and endless. In You, I totally trust. Amen.

SEPTEMBER 16: BELIEVE WHEN YOU ASK

Believe that God will answer when you ask; then
observe how faithfully He performs the task!

James 1:6 (NIV) says, "But when he asks, he must believe and not
doubt, because he who doubts is like a wave of the sea, blown and
tossed by the wind."

God is our wonderful Provider. When you pray, are you assured
that the Lord will answer? Do you really believe, or do you doubt?
It is His Holy Word that gives wisdom that draws us closer to
Him. And when you do not receive, continue to ask God until
you receive or until God speaks otherwise. Never forget that He
knows what is best and He answers according to His will.

Prayer

Lord, I believe that You are able to bring to pass all that I ask of
You. Teach me to be patient and wait on You. Amen.

SEPTEMBER 17: HEAL ME, LORD

The Lord will heal His own; He will never
forsake or leave them alone!

Jeremiah 17:14 (NIV) says, "Heal me, O Lord, and I will be healed; save me and I will be saved."

Great is His faithfulness to us. No matter what sickness or illness you may be going through, the Lord is there with you. Believe and trust that He is touching and healing you at this moment.

Prayer

Lord, thank You for healing my body, soul, and spirit. I believe You are making me into a new creation in You as I pray. Thank You for Your healing and saving power. Amen.

SEPTEMBER 18: I WILL HEAL YOU

By Your stripes, I am healed, and by Your Holy Spirit, I am filled!

Jeremiah 30:17 (NIV) says, "But I will restore you to health and heal your wounds, declares the Lord, because you are called an outcast, Zion for whom no one cares."

Israel was in what appeared to be a hopeless situation. But God promised to heal Israel's wounds, and God would keep His promise. God has not changed; He keeps His promises today. He can be trusted to heal our diseases. The Lord has power to heal your body, if you would but ask Him. With God, there is no hopeless situation. By faith, cast all cares on Him.

Prayer

Thank You for healing me, Lord. I declare it to be done in the mighty name of Jesus! Have Your own way in my life. I trust You to provide all I need. Amen.

SEPTEMBER 19: THE LORD IS MY REFUGE

> Lord, You are my protection, and by Your
> Holy Spirit, I have divine connection!

Psalm 11:1 (NIV) says, "In the Lord I take refuge. How then can you say to me: 'Flee like a bird to your Mountain.'"

David vowed to put total trust in the Lord. But the fainthearted urged him to flee away to the mountain to find safety. Stand firm in your belief; put your trust in the Lord. He is greater than any mountain. Allow Him to be a high tower of protection all around you. In distress, don't run away, but run to the safety of the Savior.

Prayer

Lord, I put all my trust in You and not in humankind or this world's wisdom. I cast all my cares on You alone. You will deliver me from harm. Amen.

_____

_____

_____

_____

_____

_____

SEPTEMBER 20: BLESSED ARE ALL WHO TRUST

When God is your trust, you will not
succumb to unbelief and disgust!

Psalm 40:4 (NIV) says, "Blessed is the man who makes the Lord his trust, who does not look to the proud, to those who turn aside to false gods."

Even when there seems to be no way out, trust in the Lord, and don't let go. Call out to Him day and night. Don't put your trust in worldly schemes or those who do not seek after God.

Prayer

I trust You, Lord! No one else can supply my needs. I cry out to You. Heal my body in the name of Jesus. Amen.

SEPTEMBER 21: THERE IS NO ONE LIKE OUR GOD

> Our God is one of a kind—He has all power,
> He is holy and divine, and He is mine!

In 1 Chronicles 17:20 (NIV), we read, "There is no one like You, O Lord, and there is no God but You, as we have heard with our own ears."

By faith, we know who God is, and by experience, we know the depth of His love toward us. Not only have we heard about His power; we know firsthand that He will protect and defend His own.

Prayer

Lord, who is as awe inspiring as You? Who can compare to Your greatness? I love You with all of my heart and delight in being in Your presence through prayer. Thank You for daily blessings. Amen.

_____
_____
_____
_____
_____
_____

SEPTEMBER 22: GOD IS GOOD, AND HIS LOVE AND FAITHFULNESS ARE FOREVER

God is good; His love and faithfulness have no end.
Christ proved it when He died for our sin!

Psalm 100:5 (NIV) says, "For the Lord is good and his love endures forever; his faithfulness continues through all generations."

The goodness of the Lord lasts forever. His love has no limits or bounds. God's faithfulness flows from generation to generation. There is nothing we can do to prevent Him from loving and caring for us. We love God because He chose to love us first.

Prayer

You are my loving and faithful God. Your goodness extends from age to age. Thank You for loving and keeping me today and every day. Amen.

SEPTEMBER 23: GOD'S WORD TEACHES US GOD'S WAY

God teaches us to follow His way and guides us so we will stay!

Psalm 32:8 (NIV) says, "I will instruct you and teach you in the way you should go; I will counsel you and watch over you."

God gives us righteous people to be visible guides to His Word and way. As they follow God, we follow them, as outlined in God's Word, the Bible. As we learn God's precepts, we are commanded to obey them so that we will please the Lord.

Prayer

Lord, teach me to know Your truth and walk in it day by day. Make me to hear Your Holy Spirit as I follow His urgings from within. Amen.

SEPTEMBER 24: WHY WORRY?

Don't worry, but to the throne of grace run to God in a hurry!

Luke 12:25 (NIV) says, "Who of you by worrying can add a single hour to his life?"

When we worry, we do not trust God. Worry will not change the outcome of a situation, but trusting and crying out to the Lord in fervent prayer will.

Prayer

Lord, I will not worry, but I will trust in You today. You are my Savior and Lord, and You promised to provide all my needs. Thank You for being trustworthy. Amen.

SEPTEMBER 25: HE IS THE LIGHT

The darkness cannot penetrate God's light,
even in the darkest midnight!

In 2 Corinthians 4:6 (NIV), we read, "For God who said, 'Let light shine out of darkness,' made His Light shine in our hearts to give us the light of the knowledge of the glory of God in the face of Christ.'"

Just as physical light repels the darkness, so the light of the knowledge of Jesus Christ brings light to the human heart, and we are never the same—we see through eyes of faith. In Jesus Christ, we learn to put our trust.

Prayer

Lord, because of Jesus Christ, I am a new creation. The light of Christ resides within my heart in the person of the Holy Spirit. Father God, thank You for Jesus Christ, who died to give me light and life. Amen.

_____
_____
_____
_____
_____
_____

SEPTEMBER 26: READ THE WORD AND BE BLESSED

The Word of God will bless and give strength to pass each test!

Revelation 1:3 (NIV) says, "Blessed is the one who reads the words of this prophecy, and blessed are those who hear it and take to heart what is written in it, because the time is near."

Do you want to be blessed? This scripture verse holds the clues. Read the Word of God, understand what it says, and then obey what you've learned. We are blessed for reading His Word and for listening and responding appropriately.

Prayer

Lord, I love You, and I love Your Word. I read it and meditate upon it so that I will be moved to obey. Thank You for keeping me each new day. Amen.

SEPTEMBER 27: STUDY THE WORD TO KNOW GOD

As you study the Word, do so to learn and apply what you've heard!

John 5:39 (NIV) says, "You diligently study the Scriptures because you think that by them you possess eternal life. These are the Scriptures that testify about me."

The study of God's Word is designed to give us a deeper understanding of who Christ is. As we learn of His ways, we seek to please Him by becoming more like Him. Jesus came to do the Father's will. He did only what His Father told Him to do. Therefore, He is the role model that believers must emulate. Know God's Word and know Him!

Prayer

Lord, I want to know You the way You know me. Help me understand Your Word, so that I may apply it to my daily living and become more and more like Jesus. Amen.

SEPTEMBER 28: GOD'S COMMANDS ARE A LAMP AND LIGHT

God's Word is a lamp that gives light to fight the good fight!

Proverbs 6:23 (NIV) says, "For these commands are a lamp, this teaching is a light, and the corrections of discipline are the way to life."

The Word of God serves as a lamp that gives light to the heart and soul of a believer. It keeps us on the right path, which leads to the way of abundant and eternal life. Those without light grope in the darkness of their own way. They love darkness rather than light. Those who love light are guided to eternal life. But those who choose darkness find eternal death. Jesus Christ is the only way to life eternal.

Prayer

Father, I thank You for Your Holy Word. It provides light and peace that surpasses all human understanding. It's a lamp that illuminates the way of the righteous and banishes my fears and doubts. Your Word also provides corrective discipline on how to live a holy life.

SEPTEMBER 29: GOD'S WORD IS SWEET

God's Word is so sweet; in times of trouble, it offers a holy retreat!

Proverbs 16:24 (NIV) says, "Pleasant words are a honeycomb, sweet to the soul and healing to the bones."

The Word of God is a delight to those in trouble. When uplifting words are appropriately spoken, they encourage and soothe the soul and spirit. They provide strength in times of weakness and uplift by bringing joy to the heart. The Word of God, like the honeycomb, is sweet to the soul and provides healing to the emotions. Pleasant words provide comfort to all who receive it. As we are comforted by the Word, we are admonished to comfort others.

Prayer

Lord, I delight in reading Your Word. It gives strength to my soul and healing to my bones. I am inspired to uplift and comfort others who have a need. By your stripes, I am healed today, in Jesus's name! Amen.

_____
_____
_____
_____
_____
_____

SEPTEMBER 30: I AM HUNGRY. FEED ME, LORD!

If you are hungry, God will feed, and the
study of His Word is your title deed!

In 1 Peter 2:2 (NIV), we read, "Like newborn babies, crave pure spiritual milk, so that by it you may grow up in your salvation."

When we desire the nourishment of God's Word as a baby desires milk, we will be fed. The Word of God is nourishment for the soul, which allows us to grow from spiritual infancy into full adulthood. Open your heart as a newborn opens its mouth, so that your soul will be fed with the pure milk of the Word. Allow the Lord to feed you, and you'll not hunger again.

Prayer

Lord, I hunger and thirst for Your Word today. I desire to know You more personally and intimately. Fill me, Lord, with the basic understanding of Your Word until my desire is satisfied in You. Amen.

OCTOBER

Taste and see that the Lord is good; blessed is the man
who takes refuge in Him … The eyes of the Lord are on
the righteous and His ears are attentive to their cry.
—Psalm 34:8, 15 (NIV)

NO FRIEND LIKE JESUS

There is no Friend like the
Lowly Jesus!

Trust and believe so hope and
Peace you will receive!
For He loves us and hurts when
We do—
He is the faithful and true!

The Lord is forever and always
With you! And He will see you
Through!

Let hope and trust rise up in you,
And be assured that the Lord
Won't abandon you!

Cast your cares and concerns on
The Lord God! He cares!
For He holds you near and dear at
The center of His heart!

Shirley A. Howard

OCTOBER 1: BLESS THE LORD AT ALL TIMES

I will bless and praise the Lord all my days!

Psalm 34:1 (NIV) says, "I will extol the Lord at all times; His praise will always be on my lips."

The Lord is worthy of praise at all times, not just for what He does for us but also because of who He is. Praise flows from a thankful and grateful heart. So, never cease to give God praise.

Prayer

Lord, I worship and praise You because You are Almighty God and there is no one like You. When I open my mouth and reflect upon Your goodness, praise and thanksgiving flow forth! Amen.

_____
_____
_____
_____
_____
_____

OCTOBER 2: WAIT ON AND SEEK THE LORD

The ones who seek God are the ones with hearts humble and meek!

Lamentations 3:26 (NIV) says, "It is good to wait quietly for the salvation of the Lord."

In every life, trials and troubles will come. As we learn to trust in the Lord, we develop an attitude of patiently waiting on Him to intervene. In His Word, we grow, and in prayer, we persistently cry out to Him to save us. Patience and peace are by-products of waiting quietly before God. Present your petition to the Lord, and wait prayerfully on Him to minister His healing power in your life.

Prayer

Lord, I'm waiting on You to heal my body and change my situation. Thank You for Your faithfulness even when I fail to honor You. Right now, O Lord, I seek after You with my whole heart. I humbly bow at Your feet with great expectations. Amen.

_____
_____
_____
_____
_____
_____

OCTOBER 3: A FRIEND OF GOD

A friend of God is one who has His heart!

James 2:23 (NIV) says, "And the scripture was fulfilled that says, 'Abraham believed God, and it was credited to him as righteousness,' "and he was called God's friend.""""

Those who keep God's commands are those who love Him. Abraham (the father of the faithful) believed God, and the Lord considered him righteous, because his actions proved what was in his heart. Abraham trusted God, and he obeyed Him. Are you a friend of God?

Prayer

Thank You, Lord, for giving me a heart that seeks to be faithful and true to You. Continue to give me a mind to study Your Holy Word and commune with You in prayer. Each day, I choose to trust You and obey. Amen.

OCTOBER 4: COME NEAR TO GOD

Come near to your God and let Him take away doubt and fear!

James 4:8 (NIV) says, "Come near to God and He will come near to you."

The more you study the Word of God, the more you learn of Him. As you learn more, you are drawn closer to Him and He becomes closer to you through a bond of loving obedience. To know God (through His Word) is to love Him!

Prayer

Lord, thank You for revealing Yourself through Your Holy Word. The more I learn of You, the closer I become to You. I am so grateful to be a member of Your family. Amen.

OCTOBER 5: PRAYERS OF THE RIGHTEOUS

Prayers from the righteous ones draw them
closer to Jesus Christ, God's Son!

James 5:16 (NIV) says, "Therefore confess your sins to each other
and pray for each other so that you may be healed. The prayer of
a righteous man is powerful and effective."

This passage stresses a mutual concern for one another as
a means to combat discouragement and failure. There must be
personal confession and sincere prayer to God and one another.
Healing of the soul is what's in view here, not necessarily bodily
healing. Earnest and persistent prayer touches God's heart and
brings forth His provisions.

Prayer

Lord, thank You for Your faithfulness. Give me the ability to trust
others and the desire to keep praying for love and unity within the
body of Christ. Amen.

_____
_____
_____
_____
_____
_____

OCTOBER 6: GOD'S WORD IS FLAWLESS

God has a flawless Word; it offers salvation when it's genuinely heard!

Psalm 12:6 (NIV) says, "And the words of the Lord are flawless like silver refined in a furnace of clay, purified seven times."

The psalmist has assurance from God that He will deliver those in need (verse 5). The psalmist has confidence in God's Word, even though things didn't look as bright as what God said. We must trust the Lord regardless of how things look or seem. God will perfectly work things out for our good and His glory. God's Word is a masterpiece that He desires to cultivate in each repentant heart. His Word refines and purifies us so that we will shine like precious sliver. The Word is flawless, and in your body of clay, it is refined and purified. We become more like Christ!

Prayer

Lord, Your Word is faithful and true, and I will always believe and trust in You. Amen!

_____
_____
_____
_____
_____
_____

OCTOBER 7: GOD'S WORD IS RIGHT AND TRUE

God's Word teaches what is right and true—
it spells out what we are to do!

Psalm 33:4 (NIV) says, "For the Word of the Lord is right and true; He is faithful in all He does."

Psalm 33 is a psalm of praise that is summed up in this verse. God is dependable, reliable, and faithful in all He does. We can put all trust in Him at all times. God is just in His dealings with us. He faithfully extends His love and grace to all.

Prayer

Thank You, Lord, for Your kind care. Your Word is completely reliable. And because You are faithful, my faith and trust is totally in You. Amen.

OCTOBER 8: THE WORD OF THE LORD IS THE BREATH OF HIS MOUTH

Living Word of God, breathe on me and set me free!

Psalm 33:6 (NIV) says, "By the Word of the Lord were the heavens made, their starry host by the breath of His mouth."

God's Word is reliable, and it is life. The words that He speaks become a reality. He spoke and this world came into existence. Trust God in all He does, and when our words align with His words, we too can speak words that give life.

Prayer

Thank You, Lord, for Your awesome power. What You speak concerning my life will come to pass when by faith we both agree. Amen.

OCTOBER 9: THE PLANS AND PURPOSES OF GOD ARE FOREVER

From everlasting to everlasting, there is God—give Him your heart!

Psalm 33:11 (NIV) says, "But the plans of the Lord stand firm forever, the purposes of His heart through all generations."

No plan can override or supersede the plan of God. Nothing or no one can foil His purpose. He has a plan and purpose for your life. Your success depends on how completely you surrender to His will and way. The purpose of God's plan is to save and give abundant life from generation to generation.

Prayer

Show me the purpose that You have for me. I desire to live a life pleasing to You. Amen.

_____
_____
_____
_____
_____
_____

OCTOBER 10: YOUR NAME IS THE DECLARATION

I lift Your name on high, far above earth and sky!

Psalm 22:22 (NIV) says, "I will declare your name to my brothers; in the congregation I will praise You."

The psalmist vowed to tell the congregation of the goodness and faithfulness of God. He praised and thanked God for delivering him in times of trouble. We too can praise the Lord for His great salvation in Christ. Worship extends from a heart of gratitude.

Prayer

Lord, I am grateful for who You are, and I will praise Your name to all who will hear. I will tell of Your lovingkindness to me and my family. Amen.

OCTOBER 11: WE MATURE UNDER PRESSURE

The fire that will mature is from God, pure!

Isaiah 48:10 (NIV) says, "See, I have refined you, though not as silver; I have tested you in the furnace of affliction."

In this life, we will suffer trials and afflictions. God controls all things, and in an effort to grow us to become all He desires, He will allow afflictions to come in order to mature us and deepen our dependence on Him. Abraham was childless for many years, David was a fugitive on the run for twenty years before he became king, and Joseph was sold into slavery by his brothers. But in each situation, it worked out for their good, for the good of others, and for God's glory to increase their faith and create total dependence on Him. God has not changed; He gives us what we need to grow spiritually as He desires. What might God be doing in your life to draw you closer to Him and prepare you for greater blessing in His kingdom?

Prayer

Lord, reveal the purpose of why I'm being tried and tested in this manner. Help me to see Your will and purpose in what I'm going through. I seek your wisdom, guidance, and protection. Amen.

_____
_____
_____
_____
_____
_____

OCTOBER 12: HUMBLE TRUST

A childlike trust is a must for each of us!

Psalm 131:1–3 (NIV) says, "My heart is not proud, O Lord, my eyes are not haughty; I do not concern myself with great matters or things too wonderful for me. But I have stilled and quieted my soul; like a weaned child with its mother, like a weaned child is my soul within me. O Israel, put your hope in the Lord both now and forever."

David humbly acknowledges his trust and dependence on the Lord. He is not concerned about a deep knowledge of God ("things too wonderful"); rather he compares himself to a weaned child (age four or five), who walks trustingly beside his mother in total dependence and safety. He expresses a humble, childlike faith in God, as he encourages Israel to put their hope in the Lord forever. The church is also called to put their hope in God. He was faithful then, and He is faithful now. The Lord cannot change.

Prayer

Lord, I humbly submit my will and way to you. I totally depend on You to meet every need as You've done in the past. I will tell others of Your greatness and what You have done for me. Thank You for Your faithfulness. Amen!

OCTOBER 13: GOD'S BOUNDLESS LOVE

God's love has no limit; the magnitude of His
love goes beyond the weak and timid!

Psalm 103:11 (NIV) says, "For as high as the heavens are above
the earth, so great is His love for those who fear (reverence) Him."

God's love for those who fear (reverence) Him is so great that
it cannot be measured. He loves the saint and the sinner. He seeks
to make each person a winner through acceptance of Jesus Christ
as Savior and Lord. The heavens are above the earth, so His love
is beyond our comprehension.

Prayer

Thank You, Lord, for Your unconditional love for me. I love You
too. Amen.

OCTOBER 14: GOD KNOWS US WELL

> In the Lord, I put all my trust, for He loves
> me, though I am mere dust!

Psalm 103:14 (NIV) says, "For He knows how we are formed, He remembers that we are dust."

The love that the Lord has for us is beyond measure. He created all things for humankind to enjoy and use to glorify Him.

Prayer

Lord, I am so grateful that You know me by name. You knew me even before I was born and ordained me to be a member of Your family. Thank You. Amen.

OCTOBER 15: WRESTLE WITH GOD

> When you wrestle with God in prayer, you'll
> discover that He really does care!

Genesis 32:24 (NIV) says, "So Jacob was left alone, and a man wrestled with Him till daybreak."

Sometimes the things you want most require that you wrestle with God in prayer—not to change His mind but to reveal the sincerity of your heart and a strong desire for an intimate relationship with Him.

Prayer

Lord, I desire to know You as my friend and confidant. Therefore, I seek Your face with my whole heart. Hear and answer my prayer today, O Lord, I pray! Amen.

_____
_____
_____
_____
_____
_____

OCTOBER 16: FEED US BREAD FROM HEAVEN

By the Holy Spirit, I am led; by His Holy Word, I am graciously fed!

Exodus 16:15–16 (NIV) says, "When the Israelites saw it, they said to each other, 'What is it?'"

In the wilderness, God literally fed His people bread from heaven (the sky); they called it manna, which means "What is it?" Jesus Christ is our Bread from Heaven. He came down through forty-two generations. He was born of the Virgin Mary. He grew in stature and had power with God and men. People still ask the question: "What is it?" Jesus is the Son of God, who became human to save a sinful world. He died on a cross, was buried, and rose from the dead with all power in His hands. He sent the Holy Spirit to indwell believers, and He is coming back to receive us unto Himself. So, what is it? Jesus Christ is the only way to eternal salvation. Invite Him into your heart today!

Prayer

Thank You, Father, for Your Son, Jesus Christ! Thank You, Jesus, for sending the Holy Spirit to dwell in human hearts as we invite Him in. The plan is summarized in John 3:16. I am so thankful that Jesus is the Living Bread and the Living Word that became flesh, so that we could behold the glory of the Father. Amen.

_____
_____
_____
_____
_____

OCTOBER 17: I BROUGHT YOU OUT OF BONDAGE

Whatever situation you are in, reverence to
God is where deliverance begins!

Exodus 20:2 (NIV) says, "I am the Lord your God, who brought
you out of Egypt, out of the land of slavery."

God promised Abraham and his descendants that He would
deliver them from their captivity in Egypt, and He did. God
promised believers through His Son, Jesus Christ, to never leave
them alone, and He never will. Whatever your place of bondage
(Egypt), the Lord is able to deliver you if you trust and obey Him.
What difficulty are you having today? Give it to Jesus, and He will
work it out for you.

Prayer

Lord, I am so grateful for Your faithfulness to me today and every
day of my life. Thank You for Your kind care. I know that Your
presence is with me, and I can trust You to walk with me. Amen.

OCTOBER 18: HUMILITY PAYS OFF

A humble heart is one that's closest to Holy God!

Numbers 12:3 (NIV) says, "Now Moses was a very humble man, more humble than anyone else on the face of the earth."

A heart that seeks God is one that holds the Lord in proper perspective. God must have first place in all we say and do. Moses is said to have talked to God face-to-face. God allowed him to see His glory. The more intimate his relationship with God, the more humble he became. How close are you to the Lord? Your degree of closeness to Him will determine the degree of your humility. Humble yourself under God's mighty hand, and in His time, He will exalt you. Trust, wait, and obey!

Prayer

Lord, I desire to please You above all else. I don't seek fortune or fame; I simply desire to bless Your holy name. Like Moses, I desire to see Your glory manifested in my life and in the lives of others. Allow me to be a channel of blessing. Amen.

OCTOBER 19: MY SOUL THIRSTS FOR GOD

> My soul thirsts for the Living God, for only He can
> quench the thirst of my innermost being!

Psalm 42:2 (NIV) says, "My soul thirsts for the Living God. When can I go and meet with God?"

The psalmist longs to be in the presence of his God, who lives forever. As one thirsts for a cool, refreshing drink of water to quench physical thirst, so his soul desires to be quenched by the Living God. His delight is found in those times spent alone with Him. The psalmist anticipates the times when he will be able to meet with the Lord.

Prayer

Lord, I thank You for the time spent in communion with You. I find joy and contentment in Your holy presence. Amen.

_____
_____
_____
_____
_____
_____

OCTOBER 20: I TRUST YOU

> On You, O Lord, I fix my gaze, and when I
> cannot see, I still give You praise!

In 2 Chronicles 20:12b (NIV), we read, "We do not know what to do, but our eyes are upon You."

There may be times in life when you really don't know what to do. In such times, cry out to God in prayer, He will be there. No matter what comes your way, learn to keep your focus on the Lord. He will guide you through.

Prayer

Lord, I trust in You, put my future hope in You, and rest in the fact that You will make a way somehow. Thank You for Your faithfulness. Amen.

_____
_____
_____
_____
_____

OCTOBER 21: BELIEVE AND SEE GOD'S GLORY

Believe in the Lord, and don't doubt. He will perform
miracles that will surely bring you out!

John 11:40 (NIV) says, "Then Jesus said, 'Did I not tell you that
if you believe, you will see the glory of God?'"

Jesus raised Lazarus from the dead. Jesus revealed the glory of
the Father. Things around you may seem bleak. But God is able to
speak life to your situation—just believe! Please know with certainty
that the Lord is able to raise up from the dead any "Lazarus" that
needs resurrection in your life. Learn to trust and obey.

Prayer

Lord, let me see Your glory today! Rain down Your healing power
and grace in my life. Heal every ache and pain in my body. In
Jesus's name, I pray. Amen.

OCTOBER 22: STRENGTH FOR ENDURANCE AND PATIENCE

God gives all you need for strength and endurance to lead!

Colossians 1:11–12a (NIV) says, "[B]eing strengthened with all power according to His glorious might so that you may have great endurance and patience, and joyfully giving thanks to the Father."

We are given power by the Holy Spirit to have strength and endurance to patiently wait on the Lord in joyful obedience!

Prayer

Lord, I thank You today for the strength and power to endure each day's problems. Amen.

_____
_____
_____
_____
_____
_____

OCTOBER 23: FAITHFULNESS ENDURES FOREVER

Great is Your faithfulness, which demands total gratefulness!

Psalm 119:90 (NIV) says, "Your faithfulness continues through all generations, You establish the earth, and it endures."

Because God's faithfulness endures forever, we can trust the Lord in all His ways. He created the earth and all that is in it.

Prayer

Lord, thank You for being faithful to me and for watching over me each hour of the day. Thank You for protecting my family and friends too. Amen.

OCTOBER 24: GOD GIVES HELP IN TIMES OF TROUBLE

Put your trust in Jesus while you can; then
watch the Lord reveal His holy plan!

In 2 Thessalonians 1:7 (NIV), we read, "And give relief to you who are troubled and to us as well. This will happen when the Lord Jesus is revealed from heaven in blazing fire with His powerful angels."

God will give relief to those who trust in Him and to those who are troubled or unjustly oppressed by others. Christ will return with fire and with power.

Prayer

Lord, I trust in You and rely on You to meet every need. Prepare me for the work that must be done before You return. Amen.

OCTOBER 25: THE LORD IS MY LAMP AND LIGHT

The Lord is the lamp that lights my pathway,
giving illumination each and every day!

In 2 Samuel 22:29 (NIV), we read, "You are my lamp O Lord; the Lord turns my darkness into light."

The Lord is the lamp that transforms our darkness into His marvelous light. As we trust the Lord, He gives us knowledge and wisdom to live a life of truth and spiritual understanding.

Prayer

Thank You, Lord, for Your love and faithfulness every day. Teach me Your Word so that I gain wisdom and understanding to live a life that is pleasing to You. Amen.

_____
_____
_____
_____
_____
_____

OCTOBER 26: POWER AND ENDURANCE

God will always encourage and help us endure;
of this fact, we can be very sure!

Romans 15:5 (NIV) says, "May the God who gives you endurance and encouragement give you a spirit of unity among yourselves as you follow Christ Jesus."

God's Word gives us courage to endure this life's journey. Based on Jesus Christ's work at Calvary, we are able to build unity among ourselves through fellowship and prayer.

Prayer

I thank You, Lord, that I am able to endure and be encouraged to work toward unity because of Jesus. Reveal principles in Your Word that teach us to become one in Christ. Amen.

OCTOBER 27: LET JESUS CALM YOUR STORM

Jesus will calm the storm. Allow Him to speak to
the wind and waves and make them behave.

Matthew 8:27 (NIV) says, "The men were amazed and asked, 'What
kind of man is this? Even the winds and the waves obey Him!'"

There is nothing God cannot do. When you put your trust
completely in Him, He will move on your behalf.

Prayer

Lord, I trust You to provide all my needs today. Speak to my
situation, and change the tides of my life. I ask this in Jesus's
name. Amen.

OCTOBER 28: GOD LOVES YOU

God loves me and you! At Calvary and the empty tomb,
He came to our rescue, giving eternal life; that's true!

Malachi 1:2 (NIV) says, "I have loved you, says the Lord, but you ask: How have You loved us?"

Jesus Christ demonstrated His love for us when He died and rose from the dead, giving eternal life to all who believe and receive. There is no greater love than that. What are you willing to give to Him?

Prayer

Thank You, Jesus, for loving me so much and for keeping me every day. I will study Your Word and seek to apply it to my life each day. Amen.

OCTOBER 29: YOU ARE GOD'S REPRESENTATIVE

> Let others see the Lord God in you, and
> He will save others through you!

In 2 Corinthians 2:15 (NIV), we read, "For we are to God the aroma of Christ among those who are being saved and those who are perishing."

When the life you live reflects the attributes and love of Christ, others will see Him in your life. And they will be drawn to a saving faith in Jesus Christ.

Prayer

Lord, in all that I do, let my life reflect the sweet aroma of Your love and grace so that others will be saved. Amen.

_____
_____
_____
_____
_____

OCTOBER 30: YOU ARE THE APPLE OF GOD'S EYE

Because we are the apple of His eye, for us,
Jesus Christ was willing to die!

Zechariah 2:8b (NIV) says, "For whoever touches you, touches the apple of His eye."

God watches over His own with lovingkindness and tender mercies to guide and protect them from harm. The Lord will come to your aid in times of trouble.

Prayer

Lord, I delight in the fact that I'm never out of Your sight. Thank You for watching over me each day. Amen.

_____
_____
_____
_____
_____

OCTOBER 31: IN OUR WEAKNESS, GOD IS OUR STRENGTH

When you are weak, the Lord will make you
strong. He'll teach you a new praise song!

Isaiah 40:29 (NIV) says, "He gives strength to the weary and increases the power of the weak."

When discouragement comes, the Holy Spirit will come alongside and strengthen you in each moment of weakness. Trust Him!

Prayer

Lord, You are my strength. And all that I need, You will supply at the very moment when I need it. Thank You for Your loving care. Amen.

_____
_____
_____
_____
_____
_____

NOVEMBER

In his hand is the life of every creature and the breath of all mankind.
—Job 12:10 (NIV)

EVERYTHING IN CONTROL

Lord, You've got everything in control!
You are the Captain of my soul!

We are more precious to You than the
Purest gold!
Everything is under Your control!

You, O God, empower us to stand
Holy and bold as we go forward under the
Spirit's control!

Everything, to You, is owed, so at Your
Feet I surrender my heavy load—

You've got everything in control!

Shirley A. Howard

NOVEMBER 1: JOYFUL SONG TO THE LORD

Because the Lord is faithful to us, we can give Him all our trust!

Psalm 33:1 (NIV) says, "Sing joyfully to the Lord, you righteous; it is fitting for the upright to praise Him."

Allow the Lord to always be your song of praise. Trust in Him and refuse to doubt, for in the past, He was always there to lift the burdens that weighed you down. Even when you don't understand what is happening in your life or why things happen as they do; think on His mighty power and all that He has done for you.

Prayer

I trust You, Jesus, with all my heart. You bring peace when I am afraid. Thank You for the joy I have within today. All praise and thanksgiving is due Your name because of who You are. Amen.

NOVEMBER 2: SING A NEW SONG

Because of Jesus, I have a new song; upon Calvary's cross He hung!

Psalm 33:3 (NIV) advises us, "Sing to Him a new song; play skillfully and shout for joy."

Because of God's grace and mercy, He puts a new song in our heart that expresses the joy within. "Never alone, you are never alone!" He turns each midnight into a bright, sunny day. His love gives a song of assurance that He is beside us in each step that we take.

Prayer

Thank You, my Father, for Your grace and mercy. Your Holy Spirit keeps me each day and draws me closer to You. Amen.

NOVEMBER 3: RIGHTEOUSNESS AND JUSTICE FOR THE OPPRESSED

The Lord fights for the oppressed; therefore, I refuse to be depressed!

Psalm 103:6 (NIV) says, "The Lord works righteousness and justice for all the oppressed."

Don't allow life's problems to weigh you down. Never forget that the Lord is on your side, working behind the scenes to attend to your deepest needs. As you daily trust in Him, He lifts the burdens from your heart. Allow Him to replace them with His peace and love.

Prayer

Thank You, my dear Heavenly Father, for attending to my needs in times of stress and oppression. I will not worry, but I will trust in Your unfailing love. Amen.

NOVEMBER 4: BE HOLY UNTO ME

Be holy and devoted, and by God's grace, you'll be promoted!

Leviticus 20:26 (NIV) says, "You are to be holy to Me because I, the Lord, am holy, and I have set you apart from the nations to be my own."

God set Israel apart from the other nations to be His special covenant people who would reveal His goodness to the world. Presently, the Lord sets believing Christians apart from the world so they too, will reveal the goodness of His Son, Jesus Christ. When people see you, do they see Christ in you?

Prayer

Thank You, Lord, for saving me and setting me apart to reveal Your love and righteousness to the world. Each day, give me renewed strength to live for You. Amen.

NOVEMBER 5: THE LORD FIGHTS FOR HIS OWN

Because the Lord fights for His own, we must
never fear or think that we are alone!

Joshua 10:13b–14 (NIV) says, "The sun stopped in the middle of the sky and delayed going down about a full day. There has never been a day like it before or since, a day when the Lord listened to a man. Surely the Lord was fighting for Israel!"

Just as the Lord performed a miracle on behalf of Israel, He has not changed. He loves His children, and He still performs miracles today. Trust God, and He will fight your battles as you surrender your will to His. Call out to Him. He will hear and answer. Do you believe in miracles?

Prayer

Lord, I surrender my all to You. I trust You to fight for me when there seems to be no hope to succeed. Thank You for loving me. Amen.

NOVEMBER 6: HOPE IN GOD, AND GIVE PRAISE

> Don't be downcast in spirit and soul, but trust
> God and let Him lead you and control!

Psalm 42:5 (NIV) says, "Why are you downcast, O my soul? Why so disturbed within me? Put your hope in God, for I will yet praise Him, my Savior and my God."

When you are discouraged, don't give in to the moment. But think on the goodness of the Lord. Jesus is your Blessed Hope! Allow memories of His goodness to rise up in your soul. Let hope come alive in your heart, as you seek His face and trust His will. Then begin to praise with your whole heart.

Prayer

Lord, I lift You up where You belong! Only You can truly encourage my heart when I feel all alone. I need Your strength today. I am confident that it's on the way. Amen.

NOVEMBER 7: A PATH FOR MY FEET

Lord, You lead me in Your path of grace so
numerous problems I'm able to face!

Second Samuel 22:37 (NIV) says, "You broaden the path beneath me, so that my ankles do not turn."

When you trust in the Lord, whatever path you take, He promises to guide your way. He will be there to safeguard each step and to strengthen your resolve to stand firm.

Prayer

Dear Lord, my faith and trust rests in You alone. I rely on You to guide each step that I take today. Give me wisdom to walk in Your truth and not stray. Amen.

NOVEMBER 8: PRAY, WATCH, AND BE THANKFUL

I pray and watch with a thankful heart because
I know you are a kind and loving God!

Colossians 4:2 (NIV) says, "Devote yourselves to prayer, being watchful, and thankful."

This scripture chronicles the ingredients for blessings from above. Therefore, decide in your heart to commit to continual prayer, to be watchful, and to have a thankful and grateful heart to obey the Lord. Pray for yourself and others.

Prayer

Thank You, Lord, for giving me a heart that is totally committed to loving and serving You. Continue to teach me how to pray for myself, family, and others. Amen.

NOVEMBER 9: GOD WILL NEVER FORSAKE YOU

God will never forsake you; in all things, He will bring you through!

Psalm 27:10 (NIV) says, "Though my father and mother forsake me, the Lord will receive me."

Though those you trust and rely on the most may forsake you, whether intentionally or unintentionally, God will always be faithful to you. He will not abandon you. What a blessing it is to rely on God's faithfulness.

Prayer

In You, O Lord, I have total trust. Thank You for the calm assurance in knowing that You are always near! Amen.

NOVEMBER 10: COMFORT FOR GOD'S PEOPLE

God will comfort us, when in Him we put our total trust!

Isaiah 40:1 (NIV) says, "Comfort, comfort, my People, says Your God."

The Lord spoke these words to the Israelites as their time of trials and tests were just about over. He repeated the word comfort for emphasis, to reassure them that He had not abandoned them and that He was with them in their time of trouble and would not forsake them. He offers the same assurance to believers today. Find comfort from the Lord in whatever trial you may be experiencing.

Prayer

Lord, I trust in You to see me through each step of my journey, no matter what comes or goes. Thank You for Your continued love and care. Amen.

NOVEMBER 11: REASON TOGETHER

When the Lord calls, at His feet we will fall!

Isaiah 1:18a (NIV) says, "Come now, Let us reason together says the Lord."

The Lord invites us to enter into a dialogue with Him. Because we are His own, we are privileged to come into His holy presence with thanksgiving, praise, and petitions. We are allowed to come boldly and holy with assurance that when we speak, God hears, and when He hears, He will answer in His time.

Prayer

Thank You, Lord, for the divine invitation to worship, praise, and make requests of You. We are grateful for Your love and concern for our welfare. Amen.

NOVEMBER 12: LORD, YOU CALL TO RIGHTEOUSNESS AND LIGHT

You call and take my hand; You reveal to me Your holy plan!

Isaiah 42:6 (NIV) says, "I, the Lord, have called you in righteousness; I will take hold of your hand. I will keep you and will make you to be a covenant for the people and a light for the gentiles."

The Lord spoke these words to Israel to remind them of the great privilege and responsibility bestowed upon them. Like Israel, we are a chosen people. And we too are called to righteousness and to take hold of His hand. We are commissioned to be light in a dark world so that the world will see the light and be drawn to it. Are you letting your light shine?

Prayer

Lord, keep me near Your heart. Continue to uphold me in Your righteousness and keep me steadfast in leading others to Your wonderful saving light. Amen.

_____

_____

_____

_____

_____

NOVEMBER 13: GOD IS WITH YOU AND HE UPHOLDS YOU

In Christ, you are not alone; He will strengthen
and uphold you until the trouble is gone!

Isaiah 41:10 (NIV) says, "So do not fear, for I am with you; do not
be dismayed, for I am your God. I will strengthen you and help
you; I will uphold you with my righteous right hand."

Because we belong to the Lord, we do not have to fear difficult
times. He promised to be with us and provide our needs. He will
give strength, comfort, and healing. Trust in Him and believe!

Prayer

Thank You that I have nothing to fear in times of trouble. You are
with me to strengthen and comfort me when in distress. Heal my
body today, in Jesus's name I pray. Amen.

_____
_____
_____
_____
_____

NOVEMBER 14: A FULL LIFE IN CHRIST

In Jesus Christ, I have a full life because, for me, He gave His life!

John 10:10 (NIV) says, "The thief comes only to steal and kill and destroy; I have come that they may have life, and have it to the full."

People who steal are concerned only about themselves and their needs at the expense of others. Jesus Christ came not to take for Himself but to give of Himself for our sake, even to death on the cross. He sacrificed so that we could have life to the full. Are you living a full life?

Prayer

Thank You, Jesus, for loving me so much. You made such a great sacrifice for me. All I have, I owe to You. Therefore, I offer my life back to You. I love You! Amen.

_____
_____
_____
_____
_____
_____

NOVEMBER 15: COME TO ME AND FIND REST

We are invited to come to the Lord to find rest; as
we seek His wisdom, we will find our quest!

Matthew 11:28–29 (NIV) says, "Come to me, all you who are
weary and burdened and I will give you rest. Take my yoke upon
you and learn from me … you will find rest for your souls."

When you are burdened down with the problems and cares
of this world, there is a way out. Jesus invites all who are weary to
come to Him, and He will handle their cares and give peace and
sweet rest. Jesus is waiting on you!

Prayer

Lord, I cast all my cares and concerns on You today. I cannot handle
them on my own. I trust you to give me peace of mind, physical
strength, and sweet rest. Amen.

NOVEMBER 16: COMFORT GIVEN TO COMFORT OTHERS

God comforts us in our troubles so that we may comfort
others in their distress—this is the real test!

Second Corinthians 1:3–4 (NIV) says, "Praise be to the God and
Father of our Lord Jesus Christ, the Father of compassion and the
God of all comfort, who comforts us in all our troubles, so that we
can comfort those in any trouble with the comfort we ourselves
have received from God."

We praise the Lord because He is the God of all comfort. He
comforts us in our times of need to teach us how to comfort others
in their times of trouble. Share God's comfort with someone today.

Prayer

Thank You, Lord, for Your comfort in all that I go through. You
encourage me in the trial I face. You empower me to share my
own struggles with others, so they will learn and experience Your
comfort too. I am so grateful for Your kind compassionate care.
Thank You for keeping me. Amen.

NOVEMBER 17: I CRIED OUT AND GOD HEARD

> When I cried, He heard! The strength and
> power to succeed is found in His Word!

Psalm 18:6 (NIV) says, "In my distress I called to the Lord; I cried to my God for help. From his temple he heard my voice; my cry came before him, into his ears."

God sits on His heavenly throne with ears attentive to our cries. In times of trouble, we call to Him for help. He hears our voice and distinguishes it from all the other voices. He attends to our cries of distress and dispatches angels to defend our cause. How great and faithful is our God.

Prayer

Almighty God, thank You for hearing my prayers. I am confident that when I cry out, You hear and answer. Thank You for everything You do. Amen.

_____
_____
_____
_____
_____
_____

NOVEMBER 18: GOD, OUR HELP AND SHIELD

Christ is our help and shield. He died and rose
from the dead so we could eternally live!

Psalm 33:20 (NIV) says, "We wait in hope for the Lord; he is our
help and our shield."

We trust in the Lord because our faith rests in no other. We
wait in hope for His deliverance because He is almighty. He is the
shield of protection that shelters us from the trials and temptations
of life. He provides our needs as He deems best.

Prayer

Lord, thank You for your faithfulness. My faith rests in You alone.
You are my present reality and my future hope. When my hope
begins to wane, You help me maintain faith. And when I can't help
myself or others, You step in to shield me from the storms of life.
Thank You, Lord! Amen.

NOVEMBER 19: INCREASED FAITH

Increased faith finds its place in applying God's
Word to life, as we run this human race!

Luke 17:5 (NIV) says, "The apostles said to the Lord, increase
our faith!"

Faith is increased by continual study and application of God's
Holy Word. Faith is strengthened by communing with the Lord
in constant prayer and living in humble obedience.

Prayer

Lord, as I study the Bible, give me a deeper understanding of You,
so that I may grow closer to You and live for You, so that I might
lead others to a saving faith in Your Son, Jesus Christ. Thank You
for continually keeping me each day. Amen.

_____
_____
_____
_____
_____

NOVEMBER 20: OUR LOVE AND HOPE IS IN YOU

God's unfailing love is beyond measure—
my will is to do His good pleasure!

Psalm 33:22 (NIV) says, "May your unfailing love rest upon us.
Oh Lord, even as we put our hope in you."

Because the Lord is our help and shield, we hopefully wait
on Him to come to our aid. We must have confident trust in His
unfailing love for us at all times. Our hope is grounded in the Blessed
Hope—Jesus Christ. As we live by faith and dispense His love, His
hope is spread abroad to those who have a desire to know Christ.

Prayer

I am grateful, O Lord, for your unfailing love and care wherever I
am. I love You and thank You for this day. Empower me to share
Your love with others. Amen.

NOVEMBER 21: HE DELIGHTS IN ME TO SAVE

My soul delights in the Lord because His delight is in saving my soul!

Psalm 35:9 (NIV) says, "Then my soul will rejoice in the Lord and delight in His salvation."

The psalmist David praised God for His kind care and protection from his enemies. The Lord causes His angels to encamp around us to save us. We need not be fearful of the unknown. The Lord is faithful to keep and protect us from harm. And because He cares, we rejoice in His salvation. Share God's love with all you meet.

Prayer

Almighty God, there is no one like You. You are able to deliver me from all I go through. I delight in serving You and will seek to please You all my days. I will tell others of Your great salvation. Amen.

_____
_____
_____
_____
_____
_____

NOVEMBER 22: YOU CAN TRUST GOD

Trust in God, obey His commands, and
keep your hands in His hands!

John 14:1–3 (NIV) says, "Do not let your hearts be troubled. Trust in God; trust also in me. In My Father's house are many mansions … And if I go and prepare a place for you, I will come back and take you to be with me."

When we trust in the Lord, we have heartfelt assurance that He is in control. As a result, we choose not to worry or fret. He knows what we need, and He will provide as we trust Him and walk in obedience to His plan for us. God has a plan for your life on earth and beyond. Scripture assures us that Christ will return for His own one day. He is not a man that He would lie. He is God alone and is capable of keeping His word.

Prayer

Lord, I will not worry or fret over things that I cannot change. I cast all my cares and concerns on You. You have already provided for my needs. Thank You. Amen.

NOVEMBER 23: SOUL SATISFIED IN HIM

My soul is satisfied even when I'm tested and tried!

Psalm 63:5 (NIV) says, "My soul will be satisfied as with the richest of foods; with singing lips my mouth will praise You!"

As choice foods satisfy the body, so the soul is satisfied in its praise and worship of God. When we worship God, praise gives vitality and purpose to life. It brings joy to the soul. Lift up your voice with heartfelt praise.

Prayer

Lord, only You satisfy my deepest desires and needs. With all that is within me, I offer You the sacrifice of praise from my lips. Amen.

NOVEMBER 24: THE LORD IS WITH YOU

The Lord is with you, and in any trouble, He will see you through!

Psalm 94:14 (NIV) says, "For the Lord will not reject his people; he will never forsake his inheritance."

What peace and assurance we enjoy in knowing that the Lord is always with us. Whatever difficulty, persecution, or suffering that we go through, we can be confident that the Lord will be with us and never leave us to ourselves. He will guide and protect us in all we face because we belong to Him!

Prayer

Lord, thank You for not leaving me alone and on my own. I am Your child, and You are my Lord and Savior. I claim every victory in Jesus's name. Amen.

_____
_____
_____
_____
_____
_____

NOVEMBER 25: BE STRONG IN THE LORD

Be strong, wait on Him, and He'll give you a victory song!

Ephesians 6:10 (NIV) says, "Finally, be strong in the Lord and in his mighty power."

Who is greater than our God? Who can overpower His authority? When we are strong in the Lord, we exercise the privilege given to us by Jesus Christ to overcome resistance. We are strengthened not just by the person of the Lord but also by His resources—grace, mercy, provision, protection, and love. Claim His resources today!

Prayer

Lord, thank You for being my power and strength to confront each obstacle that I face. In your mighty power, I find rest and the desire to press on in Jesus's name. Amen.

NOVEMBER 26: GRACE AND PEACE FROM GOD

Grace and peace from God gives strength in all I face!

Ephesians 1:2 (NIV) says, "Grace and peace to you from God our Father and the Lord Jesus Christ."

Because of grace, we have God's steadfast love toward us. His peace shows our standing in Him as a result of His grace. With His grace to lead us and His peace as rear guard to sustain us, we discover the depth of His love and strength.

Prayer

Lord, thank You for Your grace and peace, which I cannot explain or understand. I receive it all in Jesus's name. Amen.

NOVEMBER 27: GOD'S PROMISES ARE SURE

God's promises are sure; they will be obeyed by a heart that is pure!

Second Corinthians 1:20 (NIV) says, "For no matter how many promises God has made, they are 'yes' in Christ. And so through him the 'amen' is spoken by us to the glory of God."

Because God is faithful and true, His promises are certain. What God says, He will do. Jesus Christ affirms all the promises of God. Our response to Him should be "yes" and "amen" to His will and way.

Prayer

Lord Jesus, You are the Faithful and True. You came to reveal the promises of Your Father. And by faith, I claim them today, for my soul says yes to You. Amen.

_____
_____
_____
_____
_____

NOVEMBER 28: GOD'S STRENGTH WITH HIS POWER

God's strength, with His power, is available
to you each and every hour!

Ephesians 3:16 (NIV) says, "I pray that out of his glorious riches He may strengthen you with power through his Spirit in your inner being."

In Christ, we have all things good and worthwhile. We should always pray for one another. Paul prayed that the members of the church would be strong to overcome resistance in their lives and have power through the Holy Spirit based on the work of Christ within their hearts. The church of today is called to intercede for one another.

Prayer

Thank You, Lord, for Your indwelling Holy Spirit based on what Jesus did at Calvary. Because we are Your body, strengthen us to be faithful to our call of dedication and duty in serving You. Amen.

_____
_____
_____
_____
_____
_____

NOVEMBER 29: COMFORT THAT OVERFLOWS

The suffering of Christ flows, and comfort from
Him overflows, as His love and peace uphold!

Second Corinthian 1:5 (NIV) says, "For just as the suffering of
Christ flow over into our lives, so also through Christ our comfort
overflows."

As children of God, we will suffer persecution and will be
misunderstood because of our devotion to Christ. But when we
suffer for the cause of Christ, God gives us overflowing comfort
in times of need and uncertainty.

Prayer

Lord, I thank You that I am confident of whatever state I'm in,
Your overflowing comfort will fill my heart with Your peace and
love. Amen.

_____
_____
_____
_____
_____
_____

NOVEMBER 30: JESUS SENT THE COUNSELOR

On earth, Jesus's work did end, so the Spirit's work would begin!

John 16:7–8 (NIV) says, "But I tell you the truth: It is for your good that I am going away. Unless I go away, the Counselor will not come to you; but if I go, I will send him to you. When he comes, he will convict the world of guilt in regard to sin and righteousness and judgment."

The disciples were grieved that Jesus had to leave them, but it was necessary for the Father's plan to unfold. Christ's departure included His death, burial, resurrection, and ascension into Heaven. On the Day of Pentecost, the Counselor, who is the Holy Spirit and Comforter, made His dramatic entry into the Upper Room. He gave power to the 120 people in attendance. Without Christ's departure, there would have been no Gospel and no Indwelling Holy Spirit. The Counselor came to convict the world of guilt regarding sin, righteousness, and judgment. He indwells in every born-again believer. The Counselor or Holy Spirit uses us to aid in His work of sharing the Gospel message (the death, burial, and resurrection of Jesus Chris) with an unsaved and dying world.

Prayer

Father, I thank You for Your Son, Jesus Christ, who died for my sins. I am so grateful that You chose me to be a part of Your salvation plan. And I thank You for the Holy Spirit, who indwells me and gives me power to live righteously. I am humbled by the privilege to share the Good News of the Gospel with others. In Jesus's mighty name, I pray. Amen!

_____

_____

_____

_____

_____

_____

DECEMBER

Heal me, O Lord, and I will be healed; save me and
I will be saved, for you are the one I praise.
—Jeremiah 17:14 (NIV)

HEALED

By Your stripes I am healed, and the
Mighty arm of the Lord is revealed!

For by Your Holy Spirit, I am sealed
And daily filled!

To Your will and way, I continue to
Yield in spite of what I think or feel!

Lord, Your powerful Word is real, and
Of it, by faith, I live!

Beauty for ashes, I desire You to give,
And into Your holy presence I find
Solace and strength to forgive!

Healed by faith and trust in You!
You are the faithful One that's powerful
And true!

Healed because You said it!
Healed because You desired it!
Healed because God's love required!

Shirley A. Howard

DECEMBER 1: THE LORD IS GOD

God is good, and to those who trust Him,
His faithfulness is understood!

Psalm 145:9–10 (NIV) says, "The Lord is good to all; He has compassion on all He has made. All you have made will praise You, O Lord."

We have a loving and compassionate Heavenly Father. He is good to all of His creation. The Lord alone is worthy of all praise and glory. And because we know and trust His faithful compassion, we worship and praise Him with ecstatic praise every day.

Prayer

Lord, great is Your faithfulness and compassion toward me every day. I praise and lift Your name on high. Amen!

DECEMBER 2: TURN MOURNING INTO JOY

In order to turn mourning into joy, praise and
worship to God, you must employ!

Jeremiah 31:13 (NIV) tells us, "Then maidens will dance and be
glad, young men and old as well. I will turn their mourning into
gladness; I will give them comfort and joy instead of sorrow."

This verse speaks of a future time in Israel's history when God
will restore their material blessings. The church can rejoice as well.
A day is coming when we will behold Christ face-to-face, and the
sorrow and trials of this life will turn to comfort and joy. And
even now, when we turn to Jesus in humble obedience, He will
give peace and love that this world cannot understand or destroy.
Trust Him today!

Prayer

Thank You, Lord, for the faithful promises that I now claim in
Jesus's name. I also thank You for the comfort and joy I have today
as I contemplate the future in Your holy presence. Amen.

_____
_____
_____
_____
_____
_____

DECEMBER 3: A THANKFUL HEART

When you are grateful, you have no desire to be hateful!

Ruth 2:10 (NIV) says, "Ruth fell at his feet and thanked him warmly. 'What have I done to deserve such kindness …?'"

Ruth was grateful to Boaz for his kindness. The Lord is graceful and loving to us, and out of a heart of thanksgiving, we show gratitude through our obedience. To whom have you shown kindness today?

Prayer

Thank You, Lord, for Your lovingkindness today. I am so grateful for all You do. Lead me to someone to whom I may show love and kindness too. Amen.

DECEMBER 4: GOD SATISFIES WITH LONG LIFE

God sent His Son to satisfy us with long life,
but it was not without a great price!

Psalm 91:16 (NIV) says, "With long life will I satisfy him and show him my salvation."

The Lord promises a life of protection. He will rescue us from dangers, protect us from harm, and be with us in trouble. He will honor us and satisfy our souls with hope in Jesus Christ. Good health and long life are ways that the Lord satisfies the soul. Cast all your cares on Him because He cares for you.

Prayer

Lord, I thank You for life. Without You, it would not be worth living. Yes, I have some good days and some bad days, but through them all, You satisfy my soul with love, peace, and future hope that I will see You one day. Amen.

DECEMBER 5: GOD'S GRACE IS SUFFICIENT

God's grace is what you need—our body,
soul, and spirit, He'll daily feed!

Second Corinthians 12:9 (NIV) says, "But he said to me, 'My grace is sufficient for you, for my power is made perfect in weakness ...'"

God controls all things. He didn't move Paul's affliction but promised to demonstrate His power through it. We take courage in knowing that His power is limitless. Choose to depend more on God to meet your needs rather than on your own efforts. In our own weakness, we are made strong through faith and obedience in Jesus Christ.

Prayer

Lord, You are my sufficiency. I depend totally on You for my daily needs. Thank You for all You do. You teach me that it is through my weakness that Your strength is manifested so others may see and be drawn to You. Amen.

DECEMBER 6: NOT DRIVEN TO DESPAIR

We do not linger in despairs because we have a God who cares!

Second Corinthians 4:8 (NIV) says, "We are pressed on every side by troubles, but we are not crushed. We are perplexed but not driven to despair."

Trouble will surely come in this life, yet we still maintain trust in the Lord. For we never come to the end of our rope as long as we maintain hope. Allow Jesus Christ to be your Blessed Hope. Though surrounded by trouble on all sides, be assured that He will provide a way of escape. Even in the midst of confusion, you are not driven to despair. Your peace and rest come in knowing that Jesus is always there. Just believe!

Prayer

Lord, all my faith, trust, and hope rest in You. In all my troubles, You will come to my aid. Thank You for keeping me today. Amen.

DECEMBER 7: PEACE IS IN JESUS

In Jesus Christ, you will find peace when you
trust Him and hold to your belief!

John 16:33 (NIV) says, "I have told you these things, so that in me you may have peace. In this world, you will have trouble. But take heart! I have overcome the world."

Jesus spoke these words to His disciples. These words also apply to us today. We too are in Christ and in the world. But because He was victorious over the world system, we have peace through Him and have become overcomers. In Christ Jesus, we have total victory!

Prayer

Lord, thank You for the peace I have through Jesus Christ. Because He overcame the world, I too am an overcomer. Amen.

DECEMBER 8: KEEP ASKING, SEEKING, AND KNOCKING

Ask God and receive, seek and you'll find, knock and the door will be opened—for in God's Word, it is spoken!

Matthew 7:7 (NIV) says, "Keep on asking and you will receive what you ask for. Keep on seeking, and you will find. Keep on knocking and the door will be opened to you."

What has the Lord put on your heart to desire from Him? Don't stop asking and seeking but continue knocking in prayer. Keep pressing until you hear from the Lord. There is nothing that prayer can't fix, if you persist. The Lord desires that by faith, you put a demand on His power. You are His child, and you are privileged to present your petition at the throne of grace.

Prayer

Every day, O Lord, I seek after You, for my life is invested in You. You know my every need. And I trust You to do what is pleasing in Your sight, for You are my Holy Delight. Amen.

_____

_____

_____

_____

_____

DECEMBER 9: KNOW GOD, KNOW WISDOM

Godly wisdom is the tree of life—Jesus died to pay sin's price.

Proverbs 3:18 (NIV) says, "Wisdom is a tree of life to those who embrace her; happy are those who hold her tightly."

Wisdom is more than simply knowing. The foundation of knowledge is to honor and respect the Lord, who gives wisdom to all who seek His truth. The purpose of wisdom is to know Jesus as Savior and Lord. The roots of wisdom run deep and ground the one who possesses it. It deposits words of life to all who tap into it. True wisdom lies in the study of God's Word. Chase after it as you would a mountain of gold. For it brings peace and enlightenment to the soul.

Prayer

Lord, give me wisdom today, and allow it to grow more and more. Thank You for the privilege to know You more fully. I desire your wisdom so that I will become deeply rooted in Your Holy Word. Then I will be equipped to tell others of your salvation, power, and grace. I delight in the study and sharing of Your Word every day. Amen.

DECEMBER 10: STAND UP IN FAITH

By trust and faith, you can experience
God's saving and healing grace!

Mark 2:11 (NIV) says, "I tell you, get up, take your mat and go home."

Jesus spoke those words to the crippled man; he believed, obeyed, and was healed. Jesus has the power to forgive sin and heal the physical body. Stand up in your faith, pick up your hope, and walk into your healing. The mat is your testimony of what God has done for you. Tell others about how God brought you through. The Lord is waiting on you.

Prayer

Lord Jesus, You are the Great Physician. There is nothing that You can't do. I ask You in the name of Jesus to heal my body today. Amen.

DECEMBER 11: LET YOUR WHOLE BEING PRAISE HIM

Praise God with your everything—watch
Him give you a song to sing!

Psalm 103:2 (NIV) says, "Let all that I am praise the Lord may I never, forget the good things He does for me."

Take time today to reflect upon the good things the Lord does for you. A thankful heart never forgets to show appreciation for His provisions. Give God thanksgiving for all things, great or small, as He is the giver of all things. Praise Him with your whole being—body, soul, and spirit. It will fill your heart with a joyful song of praise and thanksgiving that will result in thanks-living.

Prayer

Lord, I am so grateful for the kind care and love that You give each day. Thank You for filling my heart with overflowing joy and gladness. Bless my family and others and allow them to see how wonderful You are. Amen.

DECEMBER 12: GOD'S PRESENCE IS WITH YOU

God's presence is with you; allow His grace and mercy to keep you!

Exodus 33:14 (NIV) says, "Praise the Lord, My soul, and forget not all his benefits."

God's presence is everywhere; we can have joy in knowing that wherever we go, the Lord is with us. There may be times when we do not sense His presence, but by faith and trust, we know that God is with us in Spirit. And because He is with us, we experience sweet rest. For in the Person of the Holy Spirit, God dwells in our heart. Give control of your life to Him today.

Prayer

Lord, thank You for the assurance that You will never leave me alone. I find peace and contentment in Your presence every day. Amen.

DECEMBER 13: THE LORD HEALS

When God heals, His power and majesty are revealed!

Exodus 15:26 (NIV) says, "He said, If you listen carefully to the voice of the Lord your God, and do what is right in His eyes; if you pay attention to His commands and keep all His decrees, I will not bring on you any of the diseases I brought on the Egyptians, for I Am the Lord, Who heals you."

It is through obedience to the Lord's decrees that we experience His blessings and healing. As we yield to them, we find a confident peace and assurance that no matter how things seem, we know that the Lord is working things out on our behalf. He will guide and protect His own. He heals our soul's diseases and gives a blessing that pleases!

Prayer

Lord, thank You for revealing Your power and majesty to me! Touch my body and heal me today; lead me in the path that teaches me to obey Your will and way. Amen.

DECEMBER 14: BY FAITH BE HEALED

By faith, be healed; total belief and trust in God, you should give!

Acts 14:9–10 (NIV) says, "The man listened to Paul as he was speaking. Paul looked directly at him, saw that he had faith to be healed and called out, 'Stand up on your feet!' At that, the man jumped up and began to walk."

When we believe, there is nothing impossible to achieve. Faith in God is still the means by which God chooses to heal. It is our trust in the Lord and acting on that belief that brings healing. Without faith, it is impossible to please God. Is your life pleasing to the Lord?

Prayer

Lord, I trust in You. I hope in You alone and rest in Your peace today. I am waiting on You to heal me. Lord, do it now in the mighty name of Jesus! Allow my faith to move me to it. Amen.

DECEMBER 15: PRAYERS OF FAITH

Prayers of faith are baptized in God's love and grace!

James 5:14–15 (NIV) says, "Is any one of you sick? He should call the elders of the church to pray over him and anoint him with oil in the name of the Lord. And the prayer offered in faith will make the sick person well; the Lord will raise him up."

When you are weary and discouraged and on the verge of giving up, pray in faith, believing that God will answer and you'll experience His love, grace, and healing. Intercessory prayer is a powerful tool given by God. Pray for yourself and for others; then solicit others to pray for you, too. It is in praying for others that we will receive our own healing. Believe and trust God!

Prayer

Lord, I thank You for the comfort that I find in prayer as I commune with you. Please extend Your healing touch today. I join my prayers with the prayers of the saints that others will be healed as well as I. These things I ask in Jesus's mighty name. Amen.

DECEMBER 16: CALL OUT AND BE HEALED

Call out and be healed, so the arm and
might of the Lord will be revealed!

Psalm 30:2 (NIV) says, "O Lord my God, I called to You for help
and You healed me!"

There is no task too great for Holy God. We worship and praise
the Lord for who He is! He hears the groaning of His children and
is touched by their infirmities. Because He provides every need,
we give continual praise and worship from an overflowing heart of
gratitude. He hears and responds by healing our body's and soul's
diseases. Call on the Lord, and He will surely answer.

Prayer

Lord, I worship and praise You. Minister Your healing power from
the crown of my head to the soles of my feet. Only in You, O God,
am I made complete. I cry out to You with deep longings from the
heart. Heal me today, I pray, in the name of Jesus. Amen.

DECEMBER 17: HOPE THROUGH ENDURANCE AND ENCOURAGEMENT

Endurance and encouragement inspire
hope and a viable means to cope!

Romans 15:4 (NIV) says, "For everything that was written in the past was written to teach us, so that through endurance and the encouragement of the Scriptures, we might have hope."

Jesus Christ, the eternal Son of God, is the Living Hope. Scripture is designed to teach and encourage us to press on no matter what happens. It helps us to endure, to be encouraged, and to encourage others through inspiration by the written and spoken Word of God.

Prayer

Thank You, Lord, for leaving an example of hope from the past. Your Holy Word bears witness to the reality of the hope that I have in Jesus Christ, so that no matter what I go through, I am assured that You are with me and will never leave me alone. Amen.

DECEMBER 18: THE GOOD SHEPHERD

The Good Shepherd is Jesus Christ; He died
and rose again to give everlasting life!

John 10:11 (NIV) says, "I Am the Good Shepherd. The Good
Shepherd sacrifices His life for the sheep."

Jesus Christ is the Good Shepherd. He gave His own life to
save His sheep. All who believe in Him receive eternal life. He
died that we might live. We may be tempted to go astray, but He
is forever near to guide the way. Trust Him today! He is waiting
to guide you through whatever you face.

Prayer

Thank You, Jesus, for dying for me. Because of You, I live the
abundant life here and now. One day, I'll live forever with You
in eternity. I am so grateful for saving grace and the privilege to
experience Your power and abiding love. Amen.

_____

_____

_____

_____

_____

_____

DECEMBER 19: NOTHING IS IMPOSSIBLE WITH GOD

God can do the impossible! Do you believe the impossible is possible?

Luke 1:37 (NIV) says, "For nothing is impossible with God."

What is your heart's desire from the Lord? Faith challenges us to believe and take God at His Word. Don't look at the problem, but hear what God says and trust Him. Keep your gaze on Jesus Christ, who has power to do what no other can. Without faith, it is impossible to please Him—believe and receive!

Prayer

Lord, I believe that Your Word is true and You will do all that you say. Thank You for keeping me day by day. Amen.

DECEMBER 20: GIVE THE LORD GLORY

> Give God the glory, and every chance you
> get, go tell the Gospel story!

Luke 1:46–47 (NIV) says, "My soul glorifies the Lord, and my spirit rejoices in God my Savior."

When we think on the goodness of the Lord, we too will begin to praise the Lord for all of His benefits. Take a moment to reflect upon the glorious wonder of His awesome presence. Your soul and spirit break forth with unrestricted praise!

Prayer

Lord, I thank You today for Your goodness and love toward me. Thank You for being my Savior and Lord. Amen.

DECEMBER 21: I AM GOD'S CHILD

Because I'm God's child, He will see me through each and every trial!

In Romans 8:16–17 (NIV), we read, "The Spirit himself testifies with our spirit that we are children, then we are heirs—heirs of God and co-heirs with Christ, if indeed we share in his sufferings in order that we may also share in his glory."

We are adopted into the family of God through Jesus Christ, and His Spirit lives within believers. Therefore, we are sons and daughters and heirs with Christ. We have fellowship with the Father because of the sacrifice of the Son. As we share in Christ's suffering, we also become heirs of His glory. The Holy Spirit is a witness to our new standing in Christ.

Prayer

Father, thank You for adopting me into Your family. Thank You for making me a coheir with Your Son, Jesus. I love You, and my desire is to do Your blessed will. Please allow me to experience Your nearness today in a very special way. Amen.

DECEMBER 22: A LIVING HOPE

Christ is our Living Hope; in all things, He
gives us what we need to cope.

In 1 Peter 1:3 (NIV), we read, "Praise be to the God and Father
of our Lord Jesus Christ! In his great mercy, he has given us new
birth into a living hope through the resurrection of Jesus Christ
from the dead."

We give God praise and thanksgiving for the living hope that
we have through the resurrection of Jesus Christ from the dead.

Prayer

Lord Jesus, thank You for the living hope that I have in You.
Continue to give me Your heart day by day. Help me to be a living
testimony of Your goodness. Amen.

DECEMBER 23: KNOWN BY GOD

In eternity past, You drew me with a love that would forever last!

Jeremiah 1:5 (NIV) says, "Before I formed you in the womb I knew you, before you were born I set you apart; I appointed you as a prophet to nations."

This verse describes God's call of Jeremiah into His service. Like Jeremiah, God calls you and me. Because the Lord loves us, He calls and equips us to service. What has the Lord called you to do? What spiritual gifts has He given you?

Prayer

Holy Father, I know You have chosen me to be your child and to do Your blessed will. Thank You, Lord, for choosing and strengthening me in Jesus's name. Amen.

DECEMBER 24: GOD IS ABLE TO DELIVER ME

> By faith, I know God is able to deliver me in
> His time—this is my daily paradigm!

Daniel 3:17–18 (NIV) says, "If we are thrown into the blazing furnace, the God we serve is able to save us from it, and He will rescue us from your hand, O king. But even if He does not, we want you to know O king that we will not serve your gods or worship the image of gold you have set up."

No matter what comes in life, we must seek to maintain a confident faith in God. There are no guarantees that things will turn out the way we expect or desire. But we must have a steadfast resolve that no matter what happens; we will continue to trust in the Lord for deliverance. There will be times in our lives when our faith will be sorely tried. Faith in God says that we have the answer we seek before we receive it. We trust the Lord to deliver us in His own way. How strong is your faith in God?

Prayer

Holy Father and mighty God, Your authority is above all others. I will worship and serve You all my days. I trust You to orchestrate the affairs of my life. I wait on you to deliver me. By faith, I believe that what I speak with my mouth is what I will receive from You today in Jesus's Name. Amen.

_____

_____

_____

_____

_____

DECEMBER 25: A CHILD IS BORN AND A SON IS GIVEN

God the Father gave His Only Begotten Son; only
in Jesus Christ is everlasting life done!

Isaiah 9:6 (NIV) says, "For to us a child is born, to us a son is given, and the government will be on his shoulders. And he will be called Wonderful Counselor, Mighty God, Everlasting Father, and Prince of Peace."

Here we see God's perfect example of love demonstrated toward humanity. "A child is born" speaks of Christ's humanity. "A son is given" tells how the Father gave His one and Only Begotten Son to bring salvation to the world. We see a little baby lying on a bed of hay. And angels saying, "Glory to God in the Highest, peace on earth and goodwill to all mankind; the Christ child is born in Bethlehem." He grew into the God-man to fulfill the Father's plan. He became one of us to save us. On the cross, He took upon Himself the sins of all. And every need He will supply as Counselor, God, Father, and our Prince of Peace. The unconditional love of God is revealed through the Son. Salvation, peace, and joy He brings to all who will believe and receive Him. Have a blessed and glorious Christmas!

Prayer

Lord, I thank You for Your Son, Jesus, and for Your unfailing love toward me and the whole world. Thank You for joy, peace, and love through the miracle of salvation. Amen.

DECEMBER 26: REJOICE IN JESUS

Rejoicing comes through Jesus Christ. He
gives joy this world cannot destroy!

Psalm 30:5 (NIV) says, "For His anger lasts only a moment, but
His favor lasts a lifetime; weeping may remain for a night, but
rejoicing comes in the morning!"

The Lord disciplines those He loves. His lovingkindness is
limitless and boundless toward those who love and obey Him.
His grace and mercy are forever. Seek the Lord while He may be
found. As long as the door to salvation remains open, share it with
someone else!

Prayer

Lord, I praise You for who You are and thank You for all You do.
Give me courage to witness to those You lead me to. Amen.

DECEMBER 27: RESTORE JOY

The Lord will restore and give you victory forevermore! Just believe!

Psalm 51:12 (NIV) says, "Restore to me the joy of Your salvation and grant me a willing spirit to sustain me."

As the Lord renews the heart with a new attitude, He also preserves and strengthens us in His service. And because we have a new heart and mind, we have restored joy. When we draw near to Him, He will draw near to us.

Prayer

Thank You, Lord, for a renewed mind to serve You. Fill my heart with Your peace and joy today. Give me the opportunity to witness to the lost. Bless my family too. Amen.

_____

_____

_____

_____

_____

_____

DECEMBER 28: DOOR OF HOPE

Maintain trust in the Living God and let hope fill Your heart!

Hosea 2:15 (NIV) says, "There I will give her back her vineyards, and will make the Valley of Achor a door of hope. There she will sing as in the days of her youth, as in the day she came up out of Egypt."

The Lord spoke those words to His people through the prophet Hosea. These words are relevant for the time period in which we live. Whatever you may be facing, the Lord says that what was once a valley of trouble, He will turn into a door of hope. Trust in the Lord, and He will sustain you and fill your heart with songs of gladness. Jesus Christ is our Blessed Hope.

Prayer

Lord Jesus, I put all my trust in You today. I decided to lean not to my own understanding but to totally trust You to provide every need. You are everything that I need or ever hope for. Thank you for strengthening me. Amen.

DECEMBER 29: JOY FULFILLED / FULLNESS OF JOY

Fullness of joy is found in loving and serving Jesus Christ—
His mind, purpose, and love are our sacrifice!

Philippians 2:2 (NIV) says, "Then make my joy complete by being like-minded, having the same love, being one in spirit and purpose."Without a close relation to Jesus Christ, we cannot truly know His heart. As children of God, we are at our best when we seek after the Lord. Knowing Him intimately gives birth to fullness of joy.

Prayer

Lord, You are the joy of my life, and my greatest desire is to have Your mind and heart. Teach me Your words so that I will become more like Jesus and share your love with everyone I meet. Amen.

DECEMBER 30: FAITH OVERCOMES ALL

Victory is assured when one lives by a sustaining faith that overcomes all. We know God hears and answers every call!

In 1 John 5:4 (NIV), we read, "For everyone born of God overcomes the world. This is the victory that has overcome the world; even our faith."

Because of our trust and hope in Jesus Christ, there is nothing we cannot overcome. Allow your faith and trust in the Living God to move you to a new dimension in His love. Allow your faith to move you to the resolve—in Christ Jesus, there is nothing I cannot do!

Prayer

Lord Jesus, I put total trust in You. With all my heart, I'm seeking after You every day. Thank You for keeping me today and for the assurance that I can overcome the world through faith in Jesus Christ. Amen!

DECEMBER 31: THE HUMBLE HAVE MORE JOY

When you humble yourself before Holy God,
He will teach you to desire His heart!

Isaiah 29:19 (NIV) says, "Once more the humble will rejoice in
the Lord; the needy will rejoice in the Holy One of Israel."

When the humble and needy cast their cares on the Lord, He
will step in to defend their cause. Rest in the blessed assurance that
is in Jesus Christ, the Lord.

Prayer

Lord, I cast all my cares and concerns on You. I trust You to guide
each step that I take, and I thank You that my heart is filled with
overflowing joy today. Throughout this year, You have kept Your
protective arms around me. I will continue to praise You with my
whole being for the rest of my life because You are my life! These
things I pray in Jesus's name. Amen.

CENTER OF MY JOY

Lord, You are the center of my joy!
Only You have power to rescue or
Destroy!

When troubles rush in like a flood,
I simply remember and rest in Your
Holy Word—

"I'll never leave you, nor forsake
You!"

You are the center of my joy—eternally
I'll be with You to offer up worship and
Praise!

And down the Via Della Rosa, the path
Of eternal salvation was paved!

You are the Center of my joy that none
Can destroy!

Shirley A. Howard

BLESS THE LORD

Bless the Lord, oh my soul!
Lord, Your Gospel is the greatest
Story ever told!

Thank You for saving my eternal
Soul! Your name, Jesus, I'll always
Extol!

By faith, I became a member of
Your heavenly fold!

One day, I will behold You face-to-
Face on the streets paved with
Pure gold!

I bless You because You blessed
Me first!

For within my heart and being, Your
Grace and mercy You never cease
To pour!

The more I learn of You, dear Lord,
I grow to love You more and more!

I will bless You, Lord, all the way to
Heaven's door!

Shirley A. Howard

LORD JESUS, YOU ARE

Lord Jesus, You are the reason
For my song—the inspiration for
The tune I hum!

I joyfully wait for Your deliverance
To come, though it might seem
Foolish to some!

Lord Jesus, You are the reason we
Exist; Your grace and mercy—who
Can resist?

None but the foolish, unbelieving,
And sick of heart will doubt this!

For those who know You hold You
In high regard!

Lord Jesus, I shout it to the world—
You are the reason that I live!

Forever and always thanksgiving
And praise I'll truly give for as long
As I live!

Shirley A. Howard

US REVIEW OF BOOKS

"Every Day With Jesus Devotional
God Loves You and Cares For You"
BY SHIRLEY HOWARD

"This journal may be used daily as a morning, midday, or evening pick-me-up to provide spiritual insight for your quiet time with the Lord."

Monthly inspirational poems and daily spiritual messages comprise this caringly conceived guide by author and educator Howard. The year begins with a poetic heralding:

"It's a new day and a new year.
The outcome of it is not clear—
But I will not fear, because
Christ My Savior I revere!"

As is the case with each daily portion, the entry for the first day of January includes a stirring title, a short poem or encouraging phrase, a verse of biblical scripture, a sermonette of wise words from the author herself, a prayer asking for the Lord's help appropriate to the day, and some open lines for the reader to write their own meditations based on the offering. Throughout the year, the same template is utilized. The reader may wish to move ahead to a particular date of significance, such as a birthday or anniversary of a special event, which will be easily done given the book's chronological format. As well, dates that affect society as a whole are especially noted, such as July 4th, when readers are advised to "Be of Good Courage," or this subtle but powerful offering on September 11th that reminds them that the Lord is "the shield of protection," and, therefore, they need not fear "the enemy." Not surprisingly, Christmas Day is given special attention, with thoughts from Howard that lead from a little baby lying in a manger of hay to the growth of God's chosen one who was sent to save humankind by being one of us. The year ends in this heart-centered guide with a look back at the time that has passed and an exhortation to be humble and trust in the Lord.

An ordained minister, Howard, now retired from high school teaching, has taken a particular interest in poetry as a means to convey spiritual truth and here uses it generously to enhance the work that she has created. The couplets that open each day's entries are presented to underscore that day's predominating theme. The book opens and closes with several of Howard's poetic compositions, all showing her positive stance regarding how lives can be lived and improved through scripture and Christian practice. In a brief introduction, Howard relates that she experienced a stressful situation for seven years that led her to try to rely on God's word as she invites others to do. That trying time proved to her the need for a daily, deep reminder to strengthen one's core beliefs. Through her higher education in clinical pastoral counseling and other honors, she brings to her readers a well-rooted understanding of scriptural truth and its possibility for transformation. She presents these easily accessible meditations, graced with sensitive graphics, in a sincere hope that they will influence others as she was to seek God's love and the evidence of that love in their lives. By allowing her readers to record memories and ideas arising out of the daily segments, Howard has constructed a motivational manual that can be used for both quiet, individual inspiration and lively group study.

CPSIA information can be obtained
at www.ICGtesting.com
Printed in the USA
BVHW040804160223
658491BV00015B/533